PAYTON

PAYTON

MARK SUFRIN

CHARLES SCRIBNER'S SONS

NEW YORK

Charles Scribner's Sons Books for Young Readers
Macmillan Publishing Company
866 Third Avenue, New York, NY 10022
Collier Macmillan Canada, Inc.

Printed in the United States of America
First Edition   10 9 8 7 6 5 4 3 2 1

Library of Congress Cataloging-in-Publication Data
Sufrin, Mark.   Payton.
(Charles Scribner's Sons books for young readers)
Includes index.
Summary: A biography of the Chicago Bears fullback who broke the NFL record for career rushing yards in 1984.
1. Payton, Walter, 1954–   —Juvenile literature.
2. Football players—United States—Biography—Juvenile literature.
3. Chicago Bears (football team)—Juvenile literature.
[1. Payton, Walter, 1954–   . 2. Football players.
3. Chicago Bears (football team)]   I. Title.   II. Series.
GV939.P39S84   1988   796.332′092′4   [B]   [92]   88–15751
ISBN 0–684–18940–2

P

PAYTON

PAYTON

MARK SUFRIN

CHARLES SCRIBNER'S SONS
NEW YORK

Charles Scribner's Sons Books for Young Readers
Macmillan Publishing Company
866 Third Avenue, New York, NY 10022
Collier Macmillan Canada, Inc.

Printed in the United States of America
First Edition   10   9   8   7   6   5   4   3   2   1

Library of Congress Cataloging-in-Publication Data
Sufrin, Mark.   Payton.
(Charles Scribner's Sons books for young readers)
Includes index.
Summary: A biography of the Chicago Bears fullback who broke the NFL
record for career rushing yards in 1984.
1. Payton, Walter, 1954–   —Juvenile literature.
2. Football players—United States—Biography—Juvenile literature.
3. Chicago Bears (football team)—Juvenile literature.
[1. Payton, Walter, 1954–   . 2. Football players.
3. Chicago Bears (football team)]   I. Title.   II. Series.
GV939.P39S84   1988   796.332′092′4   [B]   [92]   88–15751
ISBN 0–684–18940–2

"It all depends on what you consider greatness. Numbers alone don't indicate the greatness of a player. They don't tell if he's reached all his expectations or if he's gone beyond those expectations. I've always tried *not* to settle for the best—but to reach beyond my last performance. I'm still going. I'm still reaching. Until I reach that level I don't consider myself to be great."

He paused, then shocked the crowd around his locker:

"My goal is 15,000 yards. If Jim Brown's record happens to fall along the way, well, it falls."

Payton started for the practice field and a writer said, "I know the guy is great, but I didn't know he's crazy. Fifteen thousand yards? Hell, he's in his tenth season. He'll never do it, it's impossible."

Another writer watched Payton pass through the locker room door. "Don't bet your mortgage on it. I have a feeling about that guy. I think he can do whatever he sets his mind to."

Payton's march to the career rushing record had gone almost unnoticed. Chicago's beloved Cubs were playing for their first National League baseball pennant in forty years. In his quiet way, Payton had taken dead aim on Brown. At the start of the season he had 11,625 yards—325 behind Franco Harris, former Pittsburgh Steeler and that year with the Seattle Seahawks, and 687 behind Brown. First, Payton had what he called his "11,000-yard checkup." Both knees were arthroscoped to clean out the debris collected in nine years of punishing his body for teams far less talented than those that supported Brown and Harris.

"I've always needed motivation," Payton said, "so I decided to pass Harris before *he* set the record."

In the season's fourth game he passed Harris, who was soon gone from the Seahawks and never reached Brown's

record. After the fifth game against Dallas, Payton had 621 yards, the best start of his career. A writer asked him what kind of run he wanted against the Saints to set the record.

"I want to go up the middle, hit one guy, bounce off another and another, jump over somebody, and fight for the extra yard. I don't want to just break free around end and run unobstructed. I want it to be hard."

The day of the New Orleans game broke raw and gray, and by kickoff there was a cold drizzle. At first, the yards came grudgingly. Running in his eccentric, prancing, smashing style, Payton gained 34 yards on 6 carries. The Saints' defensive players seemed inspired to stop him from getting the record against them. But by halftime he had scored a touchdown and gained 64 yards on 15 carries. He needed only 3 to become the league's all-time rusher.

The Bears received the second half kickoff. On the first play from scrimmage Payton gained a yard. One to tie the record—2 to break it. In the huddle, quarterback Jim McMahon called, "Toss twenty-eight weak." The play was a pitchout to Payton sweeping toward the left side of the Bears' offensive formation. It was a bread-and-butter play that he had run countless times.

Denis McKinnon, the flanker, went into motion from right to left, crossing in front of Payton and Matt Suhey as McMahon shouted the signals. At the snap of the ball, left tackle Jim Covert and tight end Emery Moorehead blocked their men to the right. Left guard Mark Bortz pulled, and he, McKinnon, and Suhey led Payton into the hole. Payton skittered along, searching for that sliver of daylight, holding the ball out in front in his right hand. The only thought in his mind was *"Don't fumble!"* Just as the Saints' linebackers closed in, Payton tucked the ball away, squared his shoulders to the line, and bulled for six yards and history.

4

Club officials had talked with him about what sort of ceremony might be held when he broke the record—but very little happened when it actually occurred. The game was stopped so game officials could give Payton the ball. Bear players stampeded from the sidelines. The first to reach him was safety Tod Bell. They repeated the "high-five" leap they performed before each game. Payton's first words to Bell in that emotion-packed moment were, "You got up high for that one." The Bears mobbed him. Many Saints' players shook his hand, aware they were competing against a man already a legend.

Payton walked over to shake the hand of Saints' coach Bum Phillips. ("He's a perfect gentleman. I respect him," Payton said later.) Finally he circled the group on the field and walked to his own bench, where again he was engulfed by a swarm of players. He handed the ball to backfield coach Johnny Roland, who gave it to Pete Elliott, director of the Professional Football Hall of Fame in Canton, Ohio. The ball would be displayed until the end of the season, when Payton would get it back in return for his uniform. In a sky box, his family, ex-teammates Roland Harper and Mike Adamle, high school coach Charles Boston, and Payton's agent opened a bottle of champagne.

Payton's first thought after the play was *Get everyone off the field and maybe we can confuse them and get a quick score.* His teammates were impressed by how quickly Payton acknowledged the record and raced back to the huddle, where he said, "It's over with. Now let's go for the win." In the Bears' 20–7 victory, Payton finished with 154 yards, breaking another Brown record for most 100-yard games. Coach Mike Ditka took him out with thirty seconds to play, and the crowd gave him a standing ovation.

After the game Payton was subdued, still dwelling on the

ordeal of chasing the specter of Jim Brown, considered the greatest runner in football history.

"I've tried to conceal it for the past three weeks," he told reporters, "but there's been a lot of pressure. It's been really hard to deal with. I'm glad I don't have to do this every week. If you don't know how to deal with that kind of pressure, you can go astray."

Jim McMahon, who played with a broken bone in his throwing hand, was his usual blithe self: "I don't know if there was all that much pressure on him. We figured he could get the yards even if we blocked poorly. Walter does a lot on his own. But we did a good job pushing people around, and Walter did a good job of running the ball."

Payton added a graceful note to the postgame hullabaloo. First, he acknowledged the help and support he'd received from family and teammates and his coaches in high school and college. He then dedicated the record to four fine running backs who had died early in their careers: Brian Piccolo of the Bears, who succumbed to cancer; Willie Galimore of the Bears and David Overstreet of the Miami Dolphins, both killed in car accidents; and Joe Delaney of the Kansas City Chiefs, drowned while trying to rescue some boys. He credited them with inspiring him.

"Maybe when the season is over, I can reminisce. But the motivating factor for me has been the athletes who have tried for the record and failed, and those who never got the chance. It's a tribute to them and an honor for me to bestow the honor on them."

But he couldn't suppress his puckish humor. Told that President Reagan was calling to congratulate him, Payton grabbed the phone and said, "The check's in the mail." There was a pause on the other end. Then he heard the voice of the President: "Breaking Jim Brown's record is akin to Hank Aaron breaking Babe Ruth's home run record or

6

Kareem Abdul-Jabbar breaking Wilt Chamberlain's point total. This really is a most significant milestone. Congratulations upon it and good luck on your next 12,000 yards."

The media people were clamoring to know who he thought might break his record after his career was done. "I don't care who breaks my record once I retire—as long as it's my son."

Seattle's Franco Harris gained only 13 yards that Sunday. He remained third behind Payton and Brown and wouldn't speak to the press, saying only, "I'm very happy for Walter Payton. Leave me alone. I want to get dressed."

In Dallas, Tony Dorsett, the Cowboys' brilliant runner, said, "You can't overemphasize what Payton's done. You can't make too big a flap about it."

Payton received a $100,000 bonus from the Bears for breaking Brown's record, and the Kangaroo shoe company, whose product Payton endorsed and wore that day, gave him a $125,000, midnight blue, 12-cylinder Lamborghini Countach-S car.

In 1984, Payton won his sixth National Football Conference rushing title with 1,684 yards, for a career total of 13,634. He held twenty-one Chicago Bear records and four NFL records, with another five NFL career marks within reach. What was most remarkable was that Payton accomplished so much while still a prime runner. Most athletes are in steep decline when they set or approach career records. Payton had played for ten years, but according to Bear tackle Dan Hampton, "Walter still plays like he's trying to be the best tailback in the tenth grade. He still has the same enthusiasm." Payton was convinced he could go on for many years.

"The way you think is the way you are. And I think I'm twenty-three. I'm raising my sights to 16,000 yards."

He was asked about active players who were cranking out

1,000-plus seasons, runners like Dorsett, Earl Campbell, Eric Dickerson, and Marcus Allen.

"If I play a couple of more years and get up around 16,000 yards, hey, let them come on. Nothing's etched in stone. I told you what I wanted: not to be remembered as the best runner but as a guy who gave all he had."

Payton disclosed a secret. During the week before the New Orleans game, he had watched a television highlight film of the NFL's greatest running backs. For the first time he studied the man he was about to surpass.

"Jim Brown was big and strong and quick, and he could make the one-handed catch. Hey, that's what football's all about. That, and staying healthy. Brown never missed a game, and I only missed one, in my rookie year. We came to play every Sunday."

But when Payton's great moment came, Brown was nowhere in sight. A proud, spikey man, Brown had made much fuss about the manner in which his record was being approached—about the overall worthiness of Payton, Franco Harris, and other backs. The Bears' management felt it would be best if he didn't attend the game. Brown had threatened to make a comeback—at age forty-eight!—if Harris broke his record. He unfairly criticized Harris for often stepping out of bounds to avoid taking a hit. But he was complimentary to Payton: "Where are the gladiators now? Where are the football players who take risks? Football is about survival, but they don't take chances anymore. Walter Payton takes risks. Walter is a gladiator. He follows the code."

There were many Brown supporters who claimed that Payton's record was tainted. A remarkable athlete, Brown had set his in only 119 games; it had taken Payton 135. Brown, they said, had retired in his prime to enter movies, when he might have gone on for years to establish a record so high that Payton would only be passing its mid-range by now. The myth had grown that Brown could never possibly be injured, that every time he touched the ball he ran 50 yards. He didn't; he had bad days. He was fabulous but human.

Payton was aware that the difference in games might cloud his achievement. "I really wanted to break Brown's record last year, do it in nine seasons like he did. But the strike in 1982 messed things up."

And there were those who idolized Gale Sayers. They bemoaned their hero's terrible knee injury that limited his career to only 68 games. He was, they said, the greatest pure runner in football history. O. J. Simpson fans thought he would have had the record but for the stupidity of his first coach in the pros. In his first years with the Buffalo Bills, Simpson was wasted much of the time as a wingback, used mostly as a pass receiver or decoy. Still running well, his splendid career ended with a crippling knee injury.

Something more important than achieving the career rushing record began to happen to Payton. He had always been given his due as a fine running back. Now, however, coaches and players and serious observers of football recognized him for what he had become: the greatest football player who ever lived.

Mike Ditka, his coach and former all-pro player, gave his estimate of Payton: "Walter is the best football player I've ever seen. Period. At any position. Period. He's a complete player. He will run, throw, catch, block for you. He can kick with the best. And to play all these years with the enthusiasm he has is exceptional."

If Ditka seemed biased, John Madden's judgment was based on his long experience as a coach and football com-

9

mentator. In his book "One Knee Equals Two Feet," he compared Payton with other great players, past and present, taking all factors into consideration:

"As a runner, pass catcher, passer, blocker, durability, as well as kickoff and punt returner early in his career, occasional punter and quarterback if called on—any way you look at him, Walter Payton is the best ever."

IN HIS ROOKIE SEASON OF 1975, Payton was stripped in the locker room when former backfield coach Fred O'Connor walked in and saw him for the first time. "It looked as if God had picked up a chisel and said, 'I'm going to make me a halfback,' and ended up with Walter Payton."

"You couldn't help but notice him," said Bill Tobin, the Bears' personnel director. "He looked like a Greek god, even in street clothes."

Looking at Payton, the observer began to understand why he—alone of all the thousands of runners who preceded him—could survive thirteen seasons in the National Football League, particularly those years when he *was* the offense for inferior Bears teams, when he was all they had. They were years when players on other teams keyed on him and still couldn't stop him, when he faced defenders who were bigger, faster, and stronger than anyone Jim Brown played against.

Payton is 5-foot, 10½ inches, and 205 pounds. Mike Ditka insisted he "played like 240." His shoulders and arms are massive for a man with his frame, and his torso looks almost too taut for comfort. He has a broad back, slender waist, and a stomach of stonelike ledges. The word *unit* comes to mind when you see him, a unit of very fast strength. A magazine writer tells of interviewing Payton a week before Super Bowl XX. He patted him on the back to wish him good luck "and my hand fell away like a bird whose flight was interrupted by a brick wall. The thought of that coming at you at 4.5 speed is very unsettling."

"His strength is unusual," said O. J. Simpson. "In fact, it's amazing. He gets hit a lot—I mean really tagged—but the next thing you know he's off and running. I broke my share of tackles, but I was never in Walter's league."

Payton could bench press 400 pounds and do 700-pound leg presses. He was that rarity, a truly strong man but agile as a cat. He could playfully leap over a 6-foot, 4-inch, 250-pound assistant coach, walk 50 yards on his hands, throw and kick a football 75 yards, and catch towering punts behind his back with dazzling ease. When Bear placekickers practiced field goals, Payton stood under the uprights and threw a football at the kicked balls as they sailed over the crossbar—and was able to knock them off about 70 percent of the time.

He was a flawless example of that extremely rare breed—the natural athlete. To a magnificent degree he possessed what might be called the five requirements of that unusual species: physique, coordination, balance, toughness, and determination. And he was more, much more, than just a football player. He could pick up the basics of any sport in a few minutes and quickly excel if it held his interest.

"We get hundreds of calls from sports medicine people, orthopedic surgeons, physical anthropologists, therapists, and hypnotists who want to cut him open and find what's inside," said Fred Caito, the Bears trainer.

Sports medicine experts analyzed Payton's running style on a computer. The first thing they observed was that he rarely bent his knee when he ran. "There's not more than thirty percent flexion in the knee," said Caito. "Most running backs bend their knees at least twice as much. Many flex to a full ninety degrees." Payton's leg swing came from the hips instead. Not only did that extra leverage give him more power, it lifted much of the burden off the knee to the upper leg. It was one reason for Payton's longevity.

His relatively stiff legged motion made it easier for Payton to run on his toes, which is terribly difficult. Just try *walking* stiff legged on your toes. The backs of the upper legs tighten quickly. Payton could do it because he was astonishingly strong in the thighs, with massive hamstring muscles, and the buttocks.

"It all starts with genetics," said Clyde Emrich, the Bears' strength coach. "Any great athlete has to have the right body leverage for his sport. He has to have a better nervous system than most, low pulse beat, and low body fat. And if his sport requires speed, strength, and reaction time more than endurance, he has to have a lot of fast-twitch cells in his muscles. He has to have instinctive reflexes and excellent hand-eye coordination."

Payton, he said, came as close to the ideal as anyone he ever saw.

"When Walter went down the assembly line, everything was a chrome-plated part. It must have been like, 'Here comes Walter. Give me the top of the line.'"

"When God chose a lot of running back, he chose a lot of Walter Payton," said Johnny Roland, Chicago backfield coach and former star runner himself.

13

The most physically punishing thing any player does in the National Football League is run the football. Payton did it almost 4,000 times, almost 1,000 more than anyone in league history. The normal professional life of a running back is about four years. Payton ran for thirteen, and it was his durability that astonished other players. Gale Sayers, perhaps with a touch of envy because his own meteoric career was cut short, said: "Walter has been very, very fortunate. I know many other backs that probably got themselves into just as good a shape. But it just didn't happen for them. Walter had the luck of the draw."

Sayers was then told the number of Payton's carries. He was so startled he could only laugh at first. "It's amazing. It's as if the man upstairs said, 'Walter, you can play as long as you want to play.'"

Through the years, almost as if to challenge himself, Payton had set his goals higher. Before the 1986 season he set his sights at 18,000 yards, estimating that he could pass that milestone early in the 1989 season, when he would be thirty-five years old. He seemed to focus on achievements beyond comparisons with other football greats.

"I think Walter sees himself as competing beyond that," said Mike Singletary, Bear linebacker. "Once you see yourself as competing against more than just the next guy—once you say, 'I don't want to do better than the next guy; I want to do better than the next guy ever thought of doing'—now you're not looking to the next guy but ahead to what you want to do. You're setting your own goals."

Payton was virtually free of serious injury in his career, but when he was hurt, opponents rarely knew it. In a 1983 playoff game against the Green Bay Packers on an icy field, he played with cracked ribs and damaged knees. A running back with those injuries is about as competitive as a sprinter

14

with a broken leg. But Payton refused to sit on the bench. He carried a couple of times in the first quarter and told Matt Suhey he didn't think he could play anymore. Suhey said, "Do what you have to do." What Payton did was carry the ball thirty times in the game for 148 yards and give the Bears a 23–21 win. Suhey later said, "I couldn't believe what I was watching."

In a 1986 Monday night game against the Los Angeles Rams, Payton dislocated his big toe, a crippling injury for any running back, but particularly for Payton who cut and pivoted on his toes. By midweek he was practicing and by the end of the week he was skipping rope like a carefree kid. By game day on Sunday he was battering the Tampa Bay Bucs for 139 yards and caught passes for 69 yards. It would have been a surprising recovery for a twenty-two-year-old in his second pro season, but for a thirty-two-year-old veteran of twelve seasons it was incredible.

Before the 1984 season Payton had arthroscopic surgery on both knees to clean out pieces of bone and cartilage. "He ran kind of stiff legged all year," said Mike Ditka. But he ran for more than 1,400 yards, and even his surgeon wondered how he did it on those knees. He also played much of the 1985 season with a sore shoulder and torn cartilage in his ribs.

Payton was considered one of the best blocking backs who ever played the game according to Ditka and Madden.

"Most backs," said Gale Sayers, "myself included, feel that if they're going to run the ball twenty-five times or more in a game, why put a lot of effort into blocking. But Walter didn't think that way. That's what set him head and shoulders above other running backs—the maximum effort he put into other phases of the game."

Payton wanted to be the best at *everything*. In the film

room, he'd say to a teammate, "Hey, watch me cream this guy." One time Suhey ran for 100 yards on a day when Payton did not. Payton loved it. "It just shows I'm a better blocker than him," he said with a sly smile. He always wanted to be the best team player in the game and explained his dedication as a blocker.

"You want to show your appreciation as well as show that you're capable of doing it, not only to yourself but to your teammates. You never know what a person is thinking. They might figure—all he wants to do is run with the ball. But once they know that's not the case, it makes them feel a lot better and it makes their job a lot easier."

He had little patience for running backs with a narrower idea of their job. "I'm not going to name names, but there are running backs I wouldn't want to run with in the same backfield, because all they care about is carrying the ball."

"Payton's rushing yards are probably the most overrated element of his play," said an NFL referee. "For instance, there is no better blocker in the league. None. He flattens linebackers. He knocks down ends. He attacks nose tackles. You have to be down on the field to appreciate what a bull this guy is, how determined he is."

To focus only on Payton's running is to blur the fact that when he played he was the best athlete in football, if not all sports. In pro football's era of specialization, Payton was the last Renaissance man.

"He could play any position," said Brian Baschnagel, a former wide receiver for the Bears, "but he might have been limited at offensive tackle. He's only 5'10". What amazed me was, here's a running back, and I once saw him throw a football 80 yards, just kidding around. The most incredible thing I ever saw him do was the time he threw me a 58-yard touchdown pass. He was going down, two big linemen on

16

him, and he not only had the strength to whip the ball that far sidearm, but also the presence of mind to realize he could do it."

But it was his running that made Payton an immortal of the game. Few players have ever been as exciting to watch. A great open-field run is filled with danger every moment and brings a mounting excitement. Like a long ride on a bucking horse, it happens in open defiance of hostile attempts to end it. For years Walter Payton defied both tacklers and the odds. Greater than all of his records, more memorable than mere statistics, is the way he went about establishing them. He played football with an almost reckless fervor.

His nickname, "Sweetness"—some say for his disposition, others for his sweet moves as a college player—is a misnomer. "Toughness" would have been more appropriate. What he really liked to do was run over people. Opponents accused him more than once of going out of his way, of avoiding the open field or maybe even slowing down, just to take another shot at a defender. Payton said he was guilty.

"The big thing about defensive players is that they want to hit you as hard as they can on every play, destroy you. They're obsessed with that. And a lot of times they knock the crap out of you. My coach at Jackson State, Bob Hill, always said, 'If you're going to die anyway, die hard, never die easy. Dish it out, hit the hitter.' That's what I tried to do."

Since his days at Jackson State, Payton refused to accept the idea that as a running back he had to take hits. At the point of contact he quickly reversed roles on the defender, recoiled and delivered his helmet, shoulder, forearm, or stiffarm into the tackler. Even as he went out of bounds— something he hated to do—he knocked the defender on the head all the way. He was forever staking out his territory on the field, planting little seeds of unrest in a defense from which he might reap a long gain later.

"His style is much different than most," said Mike Ditka. "I've never seen anybody more reluctant to get out of the way of a hit. He uses that stiffarm so well, which is odd because it was almost a forgotten tool in football. He really does look to punish the guy tackling him. I don't know if that's wrong. It's different. He lasted all these years doing it. I think he likes to make the other guys know—Hey, if you're gonna deal with me, you've got a problem."

To ensure that he'd deal out as much as he received, Payton reinvented the stiffarm and introduced it to a generation of safeties and cornerbacks. "It's a recoilless rifle," said Mike Adamle, former Chicago running back and now a television sportscaster. "There are defensive backs in the league with fewer neck vertebrae because of it." Bear players relished Payton's awesome collisions with defenders who sometimes outweighed him by seventy pounds. Once he ran into a San Francisco Forty-Niner defensive end so hard the impact knocked the two apart as if they'd been shocked, after which Payton reversed his field and scored from 20 yards out. Against the Saints that record-breaking day, he bashed and crawled for every inch, dealing some furious blows en route. On one 7-yard gain he hit a safety smack in the chest and knocked him 5 yards downfield.

His running style wasn't glamorous, but it was so honest that even battered opponents came to appreciate it. Some observers, however, thought there was something childishly perverse in the way Payton enjoyed punishing tacklers. "What about the pain they've dealt out to me?" he asked. "Pain is expected on both sides of the line in this game. Everyone hurts, but you don't moan about it, you keep on playing." It was the professional's creed:

You play with a great deal of pain. It gives you pride, of the great sacrifice you can make, that you can tolerate what the ordinary man can't, mentally or physically. A football player must learn to accept pain, because if he doesn't have the discipline to endure it and continue, something is lacking in him.

On the field Payton was an electric presence, rarely at rest. He paced on the sideline before a game, head down, hands tucked into his waist, or banged helmets and shoulder pads with other players to gird for the battle. During a game he was still only when awaiting the snap of the ball, in his familiar, alert half-crouch, arms straight, hands on knees, helmet fixed straight ahead. His massive, flat shoulders taper down to a slim waist, widening a little at the hip, and pare down to powerful legs. With the strong, supple body, and all the white tape on his shoes, with only dark heels and toes visible that seemed like cloven hoofs, Payton looked like some centaur prancing around among mere mortals.

He did prance—it was one of his trademarks. As he started to one side of the line looking for an opening, the football palmed in a waving hand (to the horror of football purists!), he did a unique, straight-legged, toe-pointed, pitter-patter prance. It wasn't a showy gesture, but rather like an odd physical response to a dangerous situation—adjusting his stride to the moving mass of players, searching for the few tight spaces available to a running back in an NFL game.

What nature doled out to Payton he built up and honed over the years. He used weights, but it was a savage, off-season workout which he and his brother Eddie improvised during a scorching Mississippi summer that made him the great runner.

"In my senior year in college—Eddie was already in the pros—I wanted something to do, but I didn't want to be out

19

there all day messing around. I wanted something that could get the job done fast and give me the best results."

What the Payton brothers came up with was sprinting up and down the sandbanks and levees of the Pearl River at the hottest part of the day.

"We mastered the program," Eddie said, "but few others could do it. We had guys come from all over to train, and when they finished throwing up, all they could do was sit there. We carried more of them off than could walk away when they finished—if they finished."

The workouts did more than build up Payton's tremendous leg drive and endurance. The sand constantly shifted beneath his weight, forcing him to adjust again and again while still driving forward and upward. It simulated the physical dynamics of making a cut on a football field. Payton felt the sand helped him develop both balance and foot speed—made his feet react instantly when his eyes spotted an opening. "It made you get that next leg out and helped you not to slow down when you made a cut. You're dead if you slow down to make a cut in the NFL." When he was drafted by the Bears he kept the same training regimen. Every day in the off-season he ran up and down a 45-degree hill of loose dirt near his suburban home outside Chicago.

Payton traced his stutter-step to a day in the first grade. After school he was too restless to walk in line with his classmates while crossing the street. "I didn't understand why I had to walk behind slow people, so I took off and the teachers yelled to stop me. I used the stutter-step to keep the big eighth-graders off-balance and get away."

What began as a trigger reflex to childish terror, Payton worked into his running style. "I used it to get the edge. When the defense is coming after you, they have the advantage because they have the momentum going. They've already picked out the spot where they're going to meet you and lay a heavy lick. So I started running and then I used that stutter-step to throw off their timing. Once they had to start thinking on the run, I had the advantage."

A stutter-step might seem too trivial and subtle to consider in a game as basic as football. But the game comes down to who gets to whom more often, who's giving out the hits and who's taking them. There is an old football truism: *By the end of the game, you know who wants to play another quarter of football and who doesn't.* Walter Payton knew in his bones that he wanted to. Along with that knowledge of what the stutter-step did, he spent his time on a football field madly constructing his advantages against men of brute strength and sprinter speed. He often did it in small and subtle ways.

He did not, ever, lie down on the field after a tackle. For thirteen years and in thousands of hits—strong fleet men hurling themselves full throttle at his body—Payton never stayed down to nurse a wound. He sprang to his feet and strode back to the huddle, but not so fast that he couldn't get a breather. It was as if he hadn't been tackled so much as annoyed, distracted briefly from something he'd set out to do, something he was going to do anyway. "Why lay down?" he once said. "After the ref blows the whistle, you need all the time you can to get back and get your mind ready for the next play." Another reason, of course, was to keep that edge over his opponents, never letting them know they'd hurt him. "Keep your injuries a mystery."

Payton offered two unpleasant options to defenders—either they missed him or they didn't. His long runs were a repertory of noisy collisions only he survived, and the deft moves he made on the remaining, startled defenders. He was amazingly shifty for a so-called power back, had an ability to go with both feet planted in one direction and then quickly gather his body to pursue another.

21

Payton in his famous "stutter-step." *Courtesy of Chicago Bears*.

"He had a run against Dallas that truly amazed me," said Jay Hilgenberg, the Bears' all-pro center. "It was my rookie year and I was still on the sideline. He was running a sweep and coming right toward us. It was like he was coming right at me—and he made a move, well, it made me fall down. It was unbelievable. He stepped one way and then leaned completely back the other way, and I'll tell you his ear almost touched the ground. I had to go sit down after that. I didn't think a human being could do that."

Still, his most distinctive trait as a runner was the way he went down. Pound for pound, Payton was one of the strongest men in football. NFL Films put together a video called *Crunch Course,* a record of the game's hardest hits and hitters. Seven minutes were devoted to Payton, a running back. Asked who were the hardest hitters, he replied, "Nobody sticks in my mind. They all hit the same. I'm not going to give anyone that tribute."

Payton had another ploy to create an advantage for him and his team. Almost as a reflex action, after each carry he put the ball a foot ahead of his marked progress, got up and walked to the huddle. And each time the official moved the ball back. But Payton figured he might gain a few inches, and over the years perhaps a hundred yards or so. "It's a little thing maybe," said ex-Bear and Hall-of-Famer Dick Butkus, "but you're trying to tackle this guy all game, and you knock him down, and all of a sudden he's moving the ball up. It's like he's saying, 'Yeah, you stopped me, but I'm kind of still going.'"

However much we analyze Payton's style, to fully appreciate his unparalleled career we have to place him in the context of other great runners. We have to understand the role of the running back and what qualities make him great.

DESPITE THE INCREASE OF PASSING and its popularity with the fans, running the football is still the basis of the game. Football without running is only a kind of glorified Frisbee. A team that can't run the ball can't win in the National Football League. Pro football is at the same time the most complicated and the most brutally fundamental game man has ever played. And at its heart is the man who runs with the football.

A man can play many other sports to test his speed, skills, and coordination. But if he wants to test his courage, his ability to perform high-level skills in the face of punishment, he plays football. And it is the running back who performs the most physically punishing job in the game. He is the game's most colorful and exciting performer. The great runner is the physical leader of the offense, and he exerts his will on the game. On every carry he reveals something of himself, and the next snap of the ball could be his last.

In action, the great runners are instinctive, sensitive instruments working with almost unfathomable movement, energy, and desire. Their genius brings people to the stadium and keeps them fixed wide-eyed at their television sets. There is a primal appeal in the escape of a runner through the hazards of a defense. It is a capsule version of the hazards of life, as primal as man against the environment. The stunning long pass and acrobatic catch is only a momentary relief from the struggle. The basic fight is in the run, and that, perhaps, more than any other factor, reveals the appeal of the best runners.

The great running back is the consummate athlete. He is to football what a great bullfighter is to his sport or a jazz musician to his art—an improvisation on a classic theme, a man performing on the edge of spectacular failure or splendid triumph. It is something elemental in sport and art, and in the brief seconds of a runner's passage through jeopardy, it gives the spectator the experience of the best and worst of his own existence.

If that seems high-blown, it is no more so than critics' talk of an artist whose work symbolizes the human struggle. The running back is an artist, and running with the football is an art form. Each great runner is different. Each has portions of speed, power, shiftiness, courage, toughness, vision (his scan of the field as he breaks through the line), but combines the elements in different ways. It's what makes the great ones unique in their profession. The skill, the art, can't be taught. John Madden says, "You can coach a running back— *but you don't coach a great runner—you just let a great runner run.*"

Most running backs in the NFL have been running backs all their lives. In their backyards they ran and jumped and dodged imaginary opponents, kids who loved to have people chase them. A little later they were the first choice in a pickup sandlot game. Then they were high school and college heroes. At other positions, a player often has to adjust as an NFL rookie, but the running back does what he's always done. The instant he gets the ball, he instantly computes the angle of approaching tacklers, the ratio of his speed to theirs, the angles of his blockers, the distance from each sideline, the number of defenders still to his front. (O. J. Simpson says, "The great ones always 'run' three players in front of them.") His art, as all art, flows from being, not thinking. Some great runners confess that they sometimes welcome a blocking failure by teammates; it frees the runner from the rigid rule of the play and allows him to improvise, when he is at his best.

Americans love to rank one athlete in a sport as the best ever. When judging running backs, however, it is a fruitless exercise, given the many different running styles, the teams runners played with. Walter Payton's ranking as the best all-around football player is undisputed—by his peers, football historians, former players, sportswriters, and fans. But there have been players possibly superior to Payton as pure runners—Jim Brown, Gale Sayers, O. J. Simpson, Hugh McIlhenny, Eric Dickerson, and Ollie Matson, among others.

Payton holds almost every running record except the single season yardage, but yard totals are beside the point when evaluating football's best runners. What excites the spectator has more to do with their individual styles—how each in his own way, in a long run, gives us the same exhilaration of having just cheated eleven angry men. It is the manner of the escape that excites us. When watching a film of a long touchdown run by Gale Sayers or Hugh McIlhenny, we see them go 60 or 70 yards through the tangle of a defense, the

Payton, one of the great blockers, running interference for teammate
Roland Harper. *Courtesy of Chicago Bears.*

clawing hands and hurtling bodies, entirely unharmed. They make moves and feints and lightning lateral cuts that empty whole sides of a field so they can stroll the last 20 yards into the end zone. But every time they run they seem vulnerable, and it is that passage through danger, the manner of their escape, that thrills us.

Payton ran in a golden age of running backs: Simpson, Dickerson, Dorsett, Harris, Billy Sims, Chuck Muncie, Earl Campbell, Wilbert Montgomery, Curt Warner, Marcus Allen, Ottis Anderson, John Riggins, Larry Csonka, Freeman McNeil, James Wilder, and many others. But before them there were athletes who defined the art and importance of the running back in the transition period from the primitive mass attack to today's game.

Red Grange was the first college running back to become a national hero and the first to turn professional—in the 1920s, with the Bears.

In the mid-1940s, Steve Van Buren of the Philadelphia Eagles proved that a great runner could raise the level of a team to championship caliber.

The Los Angeles Rams traded nine good players for Ollie Matson in the 1950s. He was big, fast, and shifty, the prototype for today's physical marvels, a great pass receiver and kick returner. He was elected to the Hall of Fame the first year he was eligible.

The Bears' Willie Galimore was one of the fastest, most elegant and elusive runners who ever played the game. His life was cut short by a car crash. Gale Sayers was his clone.

The Forty-Niners' Joe "Jet" Perry was a little undersized but extremely fast and quick to the hole, shifty, consistent, and durable. He was the first runner to gain 1,000 yards in consecutive seasons (of twelve games!). His career lasted an amazing sixteen seasons—a record for running backs.

The Baltimore Colts' Lenny Moore was as fast and dangerous as anyone in the league, a great open field runner and receiver. He averaged more than 7 yards per carry three times and retired with 113 touchdowns, then the second most in NFL history.

Hugh McIlhenny, called "The King," who many think was the most exciting runner to ever play the game, played for San Francisco and Minnesota in the 1950s and early 1960s. He has been too quickly forgotten, except by connoisseurs of the run.

McIlhenny tells how he developed his frantic, shifty style, like a wild horse breaking free from a corral. As a boy he had to pass through a dark alley to go to the store for his mother. He'd run through fast and furiously out of fear of the potential danger he "saw" lurking in the shadows. He says that running with a football in the NFL is much the same. All the great runners seem to have their own alleys of fear, and what we remember about them is their distinctive ways of getting through them.

Watching Gale Sayers run was like watching a deer run through a minefield—aware of the speed and nimbleness and beauty of his escape, but afraid that the inevitable would happen. He ran like a flash and had uncanny peripheral vision or a sixth sense that allowed him to make moves on men he couldn't see. "I could see everybody on the field. A guy could be coming up in back of me and I felt him." O. J. Simpson said, "Gale could put a move on a guy coming at him from four yards behind him. No back could ever do that."

Sayers ran in a jagged pattern on a football field, almost as if he was creating a terraced hillside. Most runners decelerate when tacklers converge on them in order to make quick changes in direction or to prepare for heavy blows. Sayers always slammed on, slashing past startled opponents and jamming through turns with a stiff-legged, heel-first ferocity. He was a flushed deer running for its life, a cheetah pursuing prey at top speed. He could cut laterally without losing an inch of speed.

A Minnesota defensive back swore that as Sayers approached him one on one in an open field, "he split in two and I didn't know which to go after." Another defender insists that once he had a good angle on Sayers from behind, but "saw a pair of eyes staring at me and then he made a move and was gone." Still another was mesmerized by Sayers's whirligig moves. He said that as he was about to tackle Sayers, "he sprouted wings." Simpson, possibly among the five most explosive runners in history, says Sayers was probably the greatest pure runner. "Gale is the only runner who made moves that I wonder if I could have done. Maybe he had only five full seasons and didn't have great statistics, but all you had to do was see him. But all this ranking stuff doesn't really matter. All that great runners leave with us, anyway, are memories. Sayers may have been the best pure runner, but twenty years from now, when I think of Walter Payton, I'll feel good. And nobody can change that."

Simpson had sprinter speed and his runs were stunning in their grace and power. He created daylight out of a tangle of jerseys, and he, too, "ran scared through my career." His runs were long and curving, with a slight pull of his free arm along the air and a good body lean, cutting against the grain of the tacklers. Usually he would hesitate behind the line, and as he saw the defense swarming toward him, he saw the opening and slipped through the hole before it closed. And like most great halfbacks, he never seemed to get hit hard.

Tony Dorsett's forte is his acceleration. His runs have a

geometric look. Often he'll crab sideways along the line of scrimmage in a kind of searching saunter. Then, at the slightest suggestion of an opening, he is in overdrive like a straight shot. The first 10 or 15 yards pass so quickly beneath him, it's as if he has retro-rockets in his legs. He just flips a switch. Eric Dickerson holds the single season yardage record and is the only runner who has a chance to surpass Payton's records. He is like Dorsett, but bigger, swifter, and more durable. He is a light artillery shell fired again and again at the enemy. In the words of coach Paul Brown discussing his heavy use of Jim Brown, "If you have a cannon, shoot it!"

Brown was a phenomenon. One NFL coach calls him "an angry beast, and he never gave up, much like Payton." Brown was seemingly indestructible, a man gifted with the grace, speed, intelligence, and strength of a fictional hero. Though labeled a fullback, he carried his 232 pounds like a halfback, with a loose, shuffling gait that belied his sprinter's speed. He was content to run by opponents, but when cornered, he used his arm like a bludgeon to knock tacklers aside with a power a heavyweight boxer might envy.

His unique skill invented an offensive style. Cleveland coach Paul Brown told his linemen to push their defensive opponents whichever way the defenders chose to go, and he let Brown pick his own spot to charge through. Brown did implausible things in a sport that recognizes greatness by physically testing and punishing it. An incredible athlete, he seemed to go wherever he wanted to on the field. He was basically a power runner, not a beautiful or elegant runner, but in the end his power was beautiful to watch. He seemed to use whatever he needed at the moment—speed, brute strength, or a hip shake—and away. Recently he was asked how he wanted to be remembered. "That I was tough," he replied. He averaged 104 yards for every game he played and 5.2 yards per carry. For players with long careers, only Payton comes close: 89 yards a game and a 4.4 average per carry.

What made Walter Payton so compelling to watch is that he combined the traits of both a power back and a finesse back. "Walter has two qualities you don't ordinarily find in a running back," said Dallas coach Tom Landry, "great speed and great strength. Add great balance to that, and you have the best in the business. He always presents a special problem because you not only have to plug the hole once, you have to plug it twice because Walter keeps coming." Payton can be praised for his longevity and junkyard dog style, but he excites the way a flashy runner does. A sportswriter said, "No one so continuously generated such excitement. Payton's one of the rare players who can lose 3 yards and have the run described as brilliant."

Alan Page, ex-Minnesota all-pro tackle, played against Payton many times and gaped at his marvelous, gymnastic escapes: "I didn't think a human being could do what Walter did on one play. Some backs do it once in their lives, but he did it again and again and again." At times Payton looked as if he couldn't decide which of his talents to use. Waiting for blockers, he bounced and japped and swung his arms, then scissor-kicked before moving into the line behind them, bulling, cutting, darting. His frantic, eccentric style bothered the purists. In action he wasn't easy to categorize because he used every tool in the runner's repertory. He wasn't as elusive as Sayers, powerful as Riggins and Campbell, explosive as Brown, fast as Dickerson, Dorsett or Simpson. But he did it all, with a style that no coach tampered with. "I could make him a lot faster just by correcting his arm action," said Willie Gault, Chicago wide receiver and champion hurdler, "but it wouldn't make him a better runner."

Watching Payton run, you didn't worry for him as you might for Dorsett and other smaller backs. He was too tough and hostile and would often step right into the dark danger areas of the alley just to look for a hit and then go on. He ran with a crazy urgency. He escaped the death knell of the great runner, the dreaded knee injury that turns him into an average runner or ends a career. One reason is that he ran so often on his toes, he avoided the firm leg plant in which knees get caught and twisted.

In his thirteenth season, Payton was only a shade less the runner he was earlier in his career. No one knows whether his desire deserted him before his body did, and not many football players get to go out that way. Before the 1987 season, Mike Ditka put it in perspective: "Never being satisfied. Knowing you can do better than you already have. If you lose that desire, you may as well get the hell out. The day Walter doesn't arrive at training camp in great shape, the day he decides it's not worth paying the price in off-season, he'll no longer be effective."

The possibility of injury didn't scare Payton as much as the idea of playing with anything less than his usual intensity. He understood the protection he got from his aggression. Possibly he was more fearful of slowing down and finding what awaited him.

Payton never watched films of himself running. A writer once asked him to analyze his style. "I'm not feeling a thing when I'm running and cutting on the field. I don't even know what I'm doing. My aggression fuels my burning desire. I block out everything. I'm an *artiste*! Everything I do is spontaneous and creative." He pretended he was in a trance but really he was mocking those who try to analyze the movements of a great athlete. Then, more serious, he turned to the writer. "And I'm running for my life."

The constant comparisons between Payton and Gale Sayers seems to bother both proud men. But the debate seems endless, because both played for the same team and both are ranked in the elite of runners, along with Brown and Simpson. Sayers's fluid flatfooted style, so different from Payton's ramming, herky-jerky passage downfield, made him the most beautiful and poetic runner ever to carry a football.

"Sayers did things you could never explain," said ex-Bear Mike Pyle. "He had a sixth, seventh, and eighth sense. He didn't dance to the music; he wrote the music."

Sayers, perhaps more than Payton, seems obsessed with his ranking because he had so few years to prove his greatness. Along with Jim Brown, he was named to the NFL's Fiftieth Anniversary All-Star team. But when the Bears won the Super Bowl after the 1985 season, Sayers was less than wholehearted about his old team's success.

"It became obvious that Gale was a bit resentful of the team's success," said Pyle. "In a way, it was sad. He wouldn't even admit it was a great ballclub."

Sayers ran with brilliance on poor Chicago teams, and he could also pass and receive. It must have bothered him that Sid Luckman, a former Bears' great and Hall of Famer, called Payton "the best pure football player I've ever seen. I don't think we'll ever see anyone greater. I don't know how we could." Pyle joined Luckman on the Payton bandwagon. "Walter didn't have Gale's running ability; nobody did or will. But Payton is the greatest total football player who ever lived."

Payton is beyond splendid. You could argue all night and never give an inch, defending his right to be called the most complete athlete to ever compete in a sport that's far more collision than contact. Contact only leaves a player wondering if he was hit by a truck or a middle linebacker. Collision brings concussions, tears ligaments, rips shoulders, and turns cartilage to rice.

After seventeen years in retirement, Sayers's greatness is etched in the memories of opponents and teammates and fortunately can be seen on film. But time has faded his luster just enough that, as ludicrous as it seems, Sayers will occasionally be left on the outside when younger writers and broadcasters talk about the aristocrats, the runners who dominated their eras and entered the pantheon of all-time greats.

The arguments for each man seem endless. Sayers's supporters say Payton played on artificial turf about twelve times a year, a surface that gives a runner an extra burst of quickness. Payton ran behind far superior offensive lines than any Sayers enjoyed. Sayers also ran back punts in an era when there was no limit to the men who could go downfield before the kick and attack him. Payton, they say, also played his career on a field with narrow hashmarks and could run either way. In Sayers's time, the ball was placed closer to the sideline, which gave a "twelfth man" on defense.

Sayers must wonder what he could have been had he not suffered the knee injury, but he refuses to complain and recently said he considered himself fortunate to be ranked with the best, despite his short career. And he is always quick to praise Payton's physical genius. Luckman recalled a day on the sideline with George Halas, founder and coach of the Bears. "Sayers was running, and even George, who's seen a thousand runners, watched with awe and said, 'You can't coach that. It's a God-given talent.'" In his rookie year Sayers scored six touchdowns against the San Francisco Forty-Niners. Halas called it "the greatest game ever played by an individual." When he presented Sayers for induction into the Hall of Fame, he told the audience, "We will never see his like again."

After his knee surgery in 1968, Sayers came back the following year, a miracle in itself. But he was stripped of that dramatic ability to turn a corner and elude pursuers, was forced to become an inside runner—and still led the league in rushing. Like Payton, he knew what was needed to win. In the opinion of football experts, Payton was probably untouchable over the long haul—but for one game, one game only, Sayers was their choice. Sayers was the gamebreaker, the gazelle, the magician, the Michelangelo of runners. Payton was the blue collar worker who somehow kept his granite frame in one piece and his desire at a peak, despite so many years of carries and savage hits.

As a rookie in 1975, Payton was aware of Sayers's already legendary reputation as a Bear. In a statement he regretted his first few years, he said, "If Bears' fans will be patient, I'll give them another Gale Sayers." Later in his career he betrayed the fact that he was bothered about the comparisons. "It's not fair to compare Sayers with me. Fans only remember the great days he had. I'm still playing and they see me good days and bad."

They were different players in different eras with different styles and temperaments, and comparisons are futile. Perhaps Jimmy Brown put it best for all the men who carry the ball and are the focus of the enemy attack: "All running backs are bonded together by ties not known to those who've never carried the ball. We all have our Ph.D.'s in running."

4

Payton says that most of his boyhood memories have to do with running, in games and pranks and daredevil stunts like his favorite movie action heroes. Sometimes, he says, it was just for the sheer joy of running. All he thought about as a boy was "having fun" when "the days were long." It sounds like an American idyll—an energetic, happy kid filled with mischief, running free in the warm lazy days of a Mississippi summer.

There were few complications in his life, despite being black in the South. He was born Walter Jerry Payton on July 25, 1954, in Columbia, Mississippi, when the South was segregated. While he was growing up, the first surge of the civil rights battle made conditions a little better for blacks. His father, Peter, worked for a company that made parachutes and other military materiel for the government. He and his wife, Alyne, and their three children were a tightknit family. They lived in a three-room house, and any extra money was put aside for a new home.

Brother Eddie was three years older than Walter, and sister Pamela was the youngest by a year. Payton says, "She was lucky to be a girl because she didn't have to share all the clothes and toys like Eddie and I did." The parents were hard-working, sober, religious people, loving with their children, but they kept a tight rein on the boys. They were allowed to stay out after dark only in summertime but were told to stay within shouting distance.

Payton's street had thirteen families, all with boys, and he says it was "a kid's paradise." It was on the west side of Columbia, and he could see all of the small city from the house. There were patches of woods, a river, and much open country. Some nearby factories were perfect places to tempt kids into trouble. Walter was one of the smallest boys, but the fastest runner. "I was jumpy and excitable and always loved to be going, doing, getting into something . . . mostly mischief." He ran around the neighborhood barefoot and says he cut his foot every other day. But it never stopped him for long. Nothing was worse to him than wearing shoes and socks. Even today he wonders how a kid can run so fast barefoot. He still has a fantasy: he is running with the ball and a quick defensive back is cutting off his angle and closing in. He suddenly ejects from his shoes and accelerates "like an eight-year-old on the Mississippi clay."

There was a pickle factory near the Payton house. The boys played hide-and-seek at night among the barrels on the loading platform, laughing and pushing as they eluded the watchman. But his "first juking and escaping and skirting around and running for daylight" came the day he and a friend sneaked into a building where cotton was compressed into bales. They climbed on some bales and were having fun leaping about like dueling swordsmen. "I was Zorro." The friend jumped to a bale near the roof and stuck his head into a hornet's nest. He screamed and both boys leaped to the floor. They ran zigzag, swatting, scrambling, heads tucked into shoulders, desperate to escape the angry hornets. By the time they fled the building, Walter had been stung many times. But young boys quickly forget terror and pain, and as soon as his mother treated the stings he was off again—running.

Payton recalls his "first long gain against human pursuers." As much as any incident in his early life, it reveals his impatience, his determination, and physical genius, a moment when the latent talent became evident. It happened on one of his first days at the John J. Jefferson school, attended by students from first grade through high school. The bell rang at the end of the school day and the teacher lined up his class to walk them across the street. But Walter's mind was fixed only on one goal. He wanted to get home quickly and wasn't about to obey authority.

"I decided that once the bell rang, the teacher had no more control over me—so I took off running. She had her reasons for everyone staying together, but all I knew was that I was on my own when school was out. At least I thought so. She shouted at the other kids to stop me."

The small, fleeing figure was pursued by a mob of eager boys, now given permission by authority to chase down and tackle someone on school grounds.

"I was startled but didn't slow down. As I ran past the classes of older kids, the bigger boys tried to block my path and grab me or trip me. I just kept running faster, dodging and spinning away, stutter-stepping, keeping my balance, and running on. I made it, too, but the next day the teacher gave me a licking that wouldn't quit."

The escape gave him enormous confidence, and perhaps somewhere in the back of his mind he was becoming fearless, thinking he could outrun any kind of danger.

His mother was always nervous when he fished along a

treacherous, muddy river bank. "But not as nervous as she might have been," he says, "if she'd known what we did along the railroad tracks. She would have killed me." Every late afternoon a train pulled into the pickle plant. Walter and his friends were staked out a half-mile away. As the train swung by, they ran alongside a flatbed car and leaped aboard. The engineers were told to watch out for them, but the boys usually outfoxed them and got a free ride to the plant. Payton later realized how dangerous it was, how close they came to maiming or killing themselves. One slip and they would have fallen under the wheels. Cars were left on a siding for loading the next day, another temptation for Walter and his friends. One time a boy climbed into one of the loading chutes on a car. Walter quickly slammed the lid shut and slid a stick through so the boy couldn't get out. The boy panicked and screamed and Walter quickly freed him.

His father was a strict disciplinarian. When he was caught in some forbidden prank, his father cut a few switches, just in case some wore out. The front and back doors were shut to cut off escape. There were only three rooms in the house, and however frantic his attempts to keep from being cornered, his father caught him. "He got my mind straight." But as he says, "I was a kid who invented trouble. I never got whipped for the same thing twice." He was proud of that.

He instinctively knew, however, that even when he was whipped, his parents didn't think he was bad. "If my mother said, 'Don't go here,' or 'Don't do this,' I had to do it—not to be bad or disobey, just to learn why. And if I didn't learn, my father just gave me another reason." He was a boy searching to learn the extent of his abilities and courage, to learn as much of the world as he could by himself. His parents gave him that confidence to explore. They made their children feel loved and secure, and taught them right from wrong, wanting them to live by certain principles—though Payton admits much of it didn't sink in until later in life. If he was a mischievous scamp with his pals, he basked in the warm and loving atmosphere of the home, the intimacy and affection and caring discipline he received. It was the kind of upbringing that breeds brave, independent people who can face the challenge of the world.

As much a herd creature as he was at other times, Walter had the gift of a lively imagination and an ability to play alone. He assumed many roles—Zorro, Robin Hood, Davy Crockett, and Tarzan, among others. He ran through the woods, explored caves and climbed trees. It was all pretend—his mighty steed, the costumes and weapons, the duels and shootings—as he did battle with imaginary villains, rescued the oppressed, and righted wrongs.

"It never occurred to me that these heroes were white. I didn't care. To me they were good guys instead of bad. They were brave and daring. That's what I wanted to be."

He never had any sense of inferiority as a boy. His parents rarely put any emphasis on race but raised their children to be happy, self-confident achievers. He was a good student in grade school but one of the class clowns. The teacher put more pressure on boys like him and it made him work harder. It taught Payton the virtue of hard, serious work to achieve a purpose.

The family attended the Chapel Baptist Church, the largest in the area, and Walter's cousin was the pastor. He says he liked church, "even enjoyed the sermons—up to a point." He would have firm religious beliefs later on, but the young Walter was irrepressible. After two and a half hours of Sunday School and church, he was fidgeting, constantly asking his father the time. *Tarzan* was on television, and he

41

says, "When it got to be past 1:15 that was cutting it close. Little eight- and nine-year-olds were ready for running." The moment services were over, the boys burst into the street. Walter couldn't wait for his father to pull the car into the heavy after-church traffic and started home on his own. He tried to honor the Sabbath by walking, but his charged energy made him take giant steps, trying to land only once between each square of cement. After a while he was leaping, not walking. When the *Tarzan* program ended, the streets suddenly filled with the sound of screen doors whapping and a horde of kids running into the street with Tarzan yells. "Sunday," he remembers, "was a good day."

He was eight years old when his parents found the land they wanted and built their new home. It was on the north side of Columbia, just steps from the Jefferson school. He was a boy—like the man he'd become—who resented wasting a second in anything so ordinary as going back and forth to school. He loved the location of the new house and had his own room now. He could be home in a minute and, too often, was in the house when he wasn't supposed to be. His mother and father worked and he could always "figure out a reason" to be out of school for a while. He recalls that time as one of the happiest of his life, "but not so happy as I would be when I discovered the drums and began playing in the school band."

Drumming captivated him. He loved the big commanding sound, the beat and urgent rhythm, the sheer action of drumming. It was almost a forecast of his running style. Sayers might be likened to a clarinet, weaving its way through the melody with improvisation; Simpson a saxophonist with powerful, sinuous solos; Jim Brown a startling, brilliant, harsh trumpet—but Payton, as a runner, would definitely be a drum. He also loved the band practices, the girls, and getting out of class for rehearsals. The band traveled to give concerts, and Walter enjoyed having his world enlarged.

He tried Little League baseball but thought it took too much time from the fun of just playing around. He was too natural an athlete not to excel, however. He played Little League for three years and high school ball later on, but he never really liked baseball and to this day never watches it. It was too sedentary a sport for someone with his restlessness. He had never played any organized football, just the usual sandlot scrambles of boys his age, but his talent was too great and too evident to be ignored. Charles Boston became the head coach at Jefferson and had to pass the Payton home on his way to school. He often stopped to watch thirteen-year-old Eddie and ten-year-old Walter playing in neighborhood football games. A fine judge of talent, he saw great athletic ability in both boys. Eddie played the next year and became a star halfback, but when Walter was a little older and Boston watched him in schoolyard games, the coach was certain he would be even better.

"I'm not saying I knew back then he was going to be as great as he turned out," said Boston, "but I knew he was going to be something real special, and I'd been right before."

Walter, however, never thought much about becoming a football star; he was too involved in many other things. He loved the Boy Scouts—the uniform, even the mild discipline—but a troop ritual drew him closer to football. He realized how much he loved the game and the challenge it gave him.

"We had only about twenty-five registered Scouts in our troop, but when we had our meetings we'd draw up to a hundred kids for games of tag and football. It was great.

Forty or fifty of us would play football under one light. With twenty or more guys on a team, you weren't sure whether or not you really wanted the ball. You couldn't see it anyway. You had to listen for it whoosing through the air over the sound of a stampede of potential tacklers. Talk about running out of sheer fear. But I quickly learned that I wanted the ball all the time. We had some wild games."

On his first camping trip with the Scouts there were battles with troops from all over the area, each trying to mess up the other's campsite. One hunting-camping trip almost ended in tragedy. Jim Walker, the Scoutmaster, told a story about a man who had been decapitated "in these very same woods and still comes back to haunt the place, especially if there are a lot of people around making noise." It scared the boys silly and they quickly became silent. Walker had to go back to Columbia that night and left some older boys in charge. It was time, of course, for the others to become rowdy.

Walter and his cronies thought they might raise the ghost of the headless man and made a lot of noise. They heard a rustle in the bushes. "There's something there," a boy whispered. A figure dressed in a white sheet jumped from one bush to another. The boys quickly backed away from the campfire light and pointed their .22s at the bushes. One wondered if you could shoot a ghost, and a loud argument followed. The "creature" jumped again, moaning and growling. Suddenly the figure screamed and jumped again, and the boys opened fire.

"Wait! Stop shooting! This is Walk! It's just Walk!"

The boys thought it was a trick. Mr. Walker had gone home. But Walter thought it sounded like the Scoutmaster and shouted, "You sound like Walk. We'll quit shooting if you come out."

It was the Scoutmaster. He had tried to make the ghost

story a little too realistic and forgot he'd left the boys with rifles. In later years, Payton always got a shiver when he thought of the possible headline: BLACK SCOUT LEADER SLAIN BY SCOUTS. BODY FOUND COVERED WITH WHITE POWDER AND WRAPPED IN SHEET.

But young Walter and his friends were rascals, constantly tempting danger. One day they were playing on a railroad trestle high above the river. To cross, they had to hit each railroad tie with precise steps because the space between meant a long drop to the water or a broken ankle. They were joking about what they'd do if a train came along. There was no safe place to stand; the train would nearly touch the outside supports of the trestle. A few seconds later they heard a whistle and saw the train coming around the bend toward the bridge.

"We had to get out of there and fast," said Payton, "but we still had to take short choppy steps to hit the ties and not fall through. It looked like an old slapstick comedy, the bunch of us bop-bopping along the tracks, legs churning like pistons."

They didn't beat the train by much but, mischievous to the end, they hopped onto the back of the train. The railroad men came after them and they had to jump off. Then, as if topping off a delicious meal with a traditional dessert, they threw rocks at the train, and when it slowed they hightailed home.

Another time they were chased through the woods by hunting dogs. One boy, armed with a shotgun, said he was going back to see what breed they were. Walter and the others hid behind an embankment. Seconds later, the boy with the shotgun came flying out of the woods, shooting wildly behind him and followed by a yelping pack of hounds that chased them to the edge of town.

Young Walter was incurably mischievous and restless,

both attributes of a normal, healthy boy, and—to stretch a point—an artist. The mischievous boy tried to manipulate reality to suit his own imagination, as the artist does . . . as the runner does as he creates new patterns on the field. His restlessness was evidence of a great spirit, a need to challenge himself. But his pranks sometimes were near deadly. "I almost hung my neighbor, a kid named Cal Otis." Walter saw something on television that he wanted to try and the Otis boy agreed to help.

He climbed up a pine tree with a rope and told Cal to ride by on his bike. He was going to tie one end to a branch and drop the loop over him, yanking him off his "horse" as he had seen in a cowboy film. He didn't realize that if Cal rode by too fast, the rope would perhaps snap his neck. The agreeable friend pedaled furiously, and in Payton's words "he wound up swinging." The noose cut off his air for the moments until Walter scrambled down the branches, jumped the last fifteen feet and loosened the rope. Cal Otis didn't squeal on Walter, but he still has the rope burns on his neck.

Walter, this time playing a hostile Indian, shot at garbage men with his bow and arrow. He hunted birds with a BB gun in a field of pecan trees where a farmer kept his cows; the farmer fired at him with a shotgun more than once. His gang's hideout was in a hole dug out of an embankment surrounded by trees. They called themselves the Hole in the Wall Club and often sang lustily around a campfire. Once the flames spread to nearby bushes. They couldn't stamp it out and resorted to their usual strategy—get running. It took fire trucks to put out the blaze, which was edging toward Columbia.

PAYTON DIDN'T GO OUT FOR FOOTBALL in his freshman year in high school. He didn't want to give up the band and wasn't sure he could do both. He also knew his mother didn't want two sons playing football at the same time; "too nerve-wracking," she said. In his second year he began to have second thoughts about playing. Eddie had moved on to Jackson State College, and coach Boston said Walter wouldn't have to give up the band. If he had been forced to choose, he said, he never would have played football.

He was scared when he went out for the team. Now he was expected to produce on demand, and on a regular basis. He had never worn a football uniform before and knew little about the fundamentals of the game. The sandlot and school-yard games were fun, just improvised horsing around; but high school football, particularly in the South, was close to a religion. And he had Eddie's reputation to live with. He didn't like coaches pushing him, demanding he play with discipline, insisting he carry out his assignments on every play—when his splendid natural instincts saw other chances. Juniors and seniors knocked the new boys around, anxious to fend off any challenge to their varsity position.

Payton quickly learned a basic fact of football: The running back was fair game, the focus of punishment by the defense. And he didn't like it at all. The first time he carried the ball in a practice scrimmage against another school, he heard the thunder of linemen and linebackers converging on him—and panicked. He shifted into jackrabbit gear and ran for a touchdown. It would be in the best tradition of *The Boys' Book of Great Athletes* to say he scored for his team on his very first carry. But he ran the wrong way. Boston chewed him out, teammates razzed him, but the coach was secretly delighted by his lightning start and speed. On another play near the goal line, he missed the hole he was supposed to hit—and stopped in embarrassment. The coach never gave up on him, knew he could be better than Eddie, maybe better than any boy who ever played high school ball in Mississippi.

Early on, he demonstrated an almost finicky distaste for being tackled, as if it were a personal affront, a blow to his dignity as well as his body. Boston gave him advice later reinforced by his Jackson State coach. "If I couldn't elude a tackler, I'd give him something to remember. The hittee became the hitter. Clobber the guy who's trying to punish you." For the first time Payton began to really enjoy running. Defenders were less eager to take him on one on one. Suddenly it was the scared little halfback scoring rather than the big brute lineman making a crushing tackle.

He perfected the technique in practice and was confident he could do it in a game. He started against Purvis High, the first game of the season. On his first carry he scored on a gorgeous 65-yard run, so exultant he ran the last 20 yards backward. Later in the game he scored on a swift, punishing jaunt of 75 yards. He made the league's all-star team in his first year, was popular and already a leader on the field and in other school activities.

He is often modest about his football career but admits to bragging about his drum and cymbal playing in the band. He insists he was the best cymbal player in the state. He was featured in one number and "I banged and twirled the cymbals, all the while dancing and twisting. One time, just as I was finishing the routine, I twisted the cymbals so hard the leather straps came loose from the handles and were about to fall. I just used the centrifugal force I had going and stayed with them right to the grass, then let go and left them there as if it was part of the show." He is possibly unaware he was talking about the splendidly coordinated athlete, not the musician.

In January, 1970, Jefferson was integrated with Columbia High. The team now had twenty blacks and sixteen whites. Boston, no longer the head coach, was now assistant to Tommy Davis, a white man. The change made little difference to Payton. In his first game for the Columbia Wildcats, he scored touchdowns on runs of 65 and 95 yards. In another he scored six touchdowns and a 2-point conversion for 38 points, on his way to becoming the leading scorer in the Little Dixie Conference.

"That did it for integration," Boston said. "The people didn't see a black boy running down the field. They saw a Wildcat."

In a game against Hazelhurst High, Payton's team blew chances for an early score. The game was scoreless at the half, but opening the third quarter, Columbia had first down and goal to go on the opponent's 3-yard line. Three wide running plays failed. Coach Davis sent in a "keeper" play, where the quarterback fakes to a runner going left and then drives for the score over right guard. Boston approached Davis "as respectfully as I could" and said he was making the wrong call. "It's time for Walter." Davis agreed and young Payton went in for the touchdown.

In that game Payton learned the technique he would use so brilliantly in college and in the pros. He was hit three or four times on a long run. The first defender nearly knocked him over. He spun and put a hand out to keep from going down, but when he recovered his balance, he ran into another defender who tripped him. As he started to fall forward, a tackler grabbed him from behind. It was just enough to keep him from falling, and he shook loose and was gone. "I began to see that you can use getting hit to keep your balance."

He went out for baseball and track in the spring because the schedules didn't conflict. He played first base and batted cleanup. In track, though a high caliber sprinter, he concentrated on the field events. He set a new long jump record in the Hazelhurst Relays (20 feet, 7 inches) and then a new record in the Little Dixie meet (22 feet, 11¼ inches). He won his event in nine straight meets. He trained too intensely for the Southern Mississippi meet, suffered headaches and nose bleeds, took too many aspirins and became sick. He came in second but qualified for the state championship meet. The boy who'd beaten him in the Southern Mississippi jumped 21 feet, 11½ inches. Walter jumped 22 feet, 3 inches, and had his trophy.

By the time of the North-South all-star football game that summer, he had bids from dozens of universities but postponed any decision. He was flattered but confused by recruiters who came from all around the country to press football scholarships on him. He was urged to accept an offer from one of the major schools, the big football factories, where he would get national attention. Payton finally decided on Kansas State, a medium-sized school with a good football program, but up to the day he was supposed to leave he was uncertain.

At first he thought it was a good idea to go to a school far from home, to strike out on his own. Then he thought Jackson State was the right place, only eighty miles away, and his brother was there. The flight to Kansas State left from Jackson, and he stopped by the school to watch Eddie work out in practice. Struck by the peace and beauty of the campus, he sat in the stands with coach Robert Hill, who kept working on Payton. "I can show you that 98 percent of the guys who play football here get their college degree." Payton stared at the grueling drills in the late summer heat. He had no idea college football demanded so much. And this was only the first of the two-a-day workouts. Hill sensed his surprise. "The only way you get anything from football is to work at it. Then when you do your best, you can live with the fact that you've done all you can, whether you succeed or fail." During a break Eddie walked over and asked his brother what he was going to do. "I don't know," Walter said. But he was beginning to waver. He returned to Columbia and his parents were angry and disappointed.

"If you can't make up your mind where you want to go to school," his mother said, "I'll make it up for you. You're going to Jackson State."

Instead of fighting her, he suddenly felt at peace and his confusion vanished. The offers and the decision had come down on him too quickly, and he was happy to obey his parents and have it settled.

Jackson State played in a fast league of black schools, the

Southwest Athletic Conference (SWAC). Hill was a respected, excellent coach, who had sent players to the National Football League. Off the field, he was sympathetic, understanding, and concerned, but when he was coaching he was a tough, harsh man with a rough tongue.

He had favorite punishments for players who messed up on the field, broke curfew, or missed meetings. One of his tortures was to throw a ball high in the air and tell the culprit to catch it—as two guys hit him hard—and if he fumbled the ball he had to do it over and over again until he held on. Another was to have a player roll the length of the field. Payton said, "It twists your insides so that you can hardly eat, but the next time you think twice about goofing off." Hill also had a hatchet man to punish players who made mistakes, a burly linebacker who whacked someone with a board when he ordered it.

Hill was as rough with Payton as with the others, but he knew he had a gem and sometimes made allowances. Payton didn't start with the correct foot at the first step off the snap of the ball, but Hill didn't try to change him. Every other back had to cross over on that first step. Payton felt more comfortable picking up his lead foot first, and Hill saw how quick his burst was to the line. Instructing the backs, Hill would say, "Okay, everybody, I want you to do it this way." Then he'd barely turn to Payton. "And you, fool, do it your way."

He roomed with Eddie and another player. Eddie, he said, had just the right personality for a football player, perhaps better than his. He thought he could do anything he tried. Eddie was a star player, Walter only a super freshman prospect. He was more flamboyant than Walter, the kind of guy who'd spot a carload of girls and hold up traffic to talk to them. Walter was afraid to fool around like that until his senior year, when he learned that bending the rules a little was a way to have fun and keep the pressure off.

As happy as the brothers' relationship seemed, it would take on darker tones in the years ahead. Despite the difference in ages, there had always been competition between the two. At 5 foot 8 inches and 180 pounds, Eddie didn't start his pro career until after Walter was drafted by the Chicago Bears. "I saw how well he was doing," Eddie said with apparent seriousness, "and I *knew* I was better than him." The rivalry between the two could become strained at times, and for Eddie there was an unpleasant pattern. Whatever he did in sports in high school and at Jackson State, Walter came along a few years later and surpassed him. As verbal and outgoing as Walter was shy, Eddie compensated by always telling his younger brother what to do.

"I didn't let them fight," said Mrs. Payton, "but I do think Walter sort of resented his brother. Eddie would say, 'Let me show you how to do this,' and Walter would say, 'No, I don't want to know.'"

The brothers seem closer now. In 1987, Eddie—possibly with Walter's permission—appeared in a television commercial and newspaper advertisement for Dean, Witter, an investment company. The message: Special care is always taken investing a celebrity's money, someone like Walter Payton. But Dean, Witter gave Eddie, obviously little-known and unimportant, the same kind of attention. Paul Newman's brother was another noncelebrity who appeared in the series of commercials. But the Payton brothers will probably always be too competitive to truly let their guard down around each other. Even the family home in Jackson, where Eddie lives with his mother (their father died in 1979), is a combat zone. The fireplace mantel is stacked with trophies, but almost all of them belong to Eddie.

"Isn't that something?" said Walter. "He put all my trophies away. Or if any of mine are there, he'll say they're his. Even in that brochure he made up for our summer football camp, he used an old picture of me and a new one of him."

Eddie, who played for five different teams in his six years in the NFL, is defensive. He says he treated Walter the way he did through the years "because I didn't want him to grow up to be a wimp." It seems to be the classic older brother's line. Still, Eddie is at least partly responsible for Walter's success. He developed the fearsome conditioning program that gave Walter his endurance, leg drive, and balance.

Walter and a tight end were the only Jackson State freshmen to make the traveling squad for the first game against Prairie View in Texas. He remembers the relaxed pregame atmosphere, unlike the time before a professional game. "My first year with the Bears I felt so much pressure I used to hyperventilate . . . felt like we were on the way to the slaughter." But his first appearance in a college game was almost a disaster. He was back to receive the kickoff with another man. They were so nervous the ball fell between them, bouncing crazily. Payton alertly fell on the ball, but as he trotted to the sideline he tried to avoid coach Hill's withering look. He played only a few minutes and made some good blocks on a scoring drive. Jackson State lost 13–12 in the last second, when a Prairie View pass was tipped by a defender into the hands of a receiver who fell into the end zone.

Payton didn't get much playing time in the next few games. He was an explosive package of talent but terribly raw. His only aim, at first, was to play alongside Eddie, who was in his last year. He started the last four games, and in the season final against Alabama A & M in the Thanksgiving Azalea Classic, Payton had his first big day.

"Eddie would sweep one way and then I'd sweep the other. He scored the first touchdown, but I scored two, kicked four extra points, and was voted the game's most valuable player."

For the season, he carried the ball eighty times for 614 yards and a glittering 7.6 yards per carry. He kicked three field goals, scored seven touchdowns, and thirteen points after touchdown for 64 points, and already was a devastating blocker. It was an excellent performance for a freshman back, but as good as he was, no one foresaw what he would accomplish. Yet early the next year he equaled his entire freshman touchdown total in *one game*.

He was still the scared first year student who never broke training. "I spent most of my time covering for Eddie and trying to keep him out of trouble." In the off-season he was happy to have time for study, no curfews, and weekends at home. One of his great joys was dancing. He and a girl partner won a Soul Train contest in Mississippi but lost in the national finals. Bob Hill said, "He still swears that if he had a girl who could dance better, he could have won that national."

He recalled how Payton used dancing to ease the pregame tension. "The team would be standing in the parking lot on campus waiting for the bus to the stadium. Some guys would start playing music and Walter would dance for a good half-hour sometimes. He'd put pads on, jump up, and land on his elbows and knees. He'd do flips and everything. He was only pumping himself up, but it scared me. I couldn't stand to watch."

Payton knew he'd made a mistake by rooming with Eddie and his friend. At first he liked being with people he knew, but the constant closeness and the big brother-little brother relationship soon got on his nerves. He wished he could have roomed with strangers "so they would have been more considerate and vice versa." For the next three years he roomed with Rod Phillips, who later played for the Los Angeles Rams.

In 1972, his sophomore year, Payton had the greatest individual performance in the history of the National Collegiate Athletic Association (NCAA), the governing body for college athletics. In the season's second game against Lane College, he scored seven touchdowns and ran two 2-point conversions for 46 points! Lane was crushed 72–0, and some people downgraded Payton's feat because Lane was a small school with a weak team. The Lane coach, however, was generous. "I don't care if he scored seven touchdowns in the schoolyard, it was damn fine running. We've stopped other good runners in this conference, but we couldn't stop him." Jackson State tied Grambling for the conference title. Payton played in eight games, with 124 carries for 781 yards, an average of 6.2 yards per carry. He scored 16 touchdowns and 21 points on conversions, both kicking and running, for a total of 117 points—the second highest in the nation.

In the spring of 1973 Payton met the woman he would marry, Connie Norwood, a New Orleans high school senior. She was visiting her aunt, a student at Jackson State. Coach Hill, a friend of Connie's aunt, suggested that Connie go out with Payton because he seemed more mature than the other young men and didn't run around. Payton had gone with only one girl in college, but that relationship had ended. On his first date with Connie he took her to a local nightclub. They spent a great deal of time together in the few days she was there and "we seemed to click." He was terribly lonesome when she left, and they called and wrote often. Then good luck brought them together.

Ed "Too Tall" Jones of Tennessee State, a SWAC school,

Payton and his wife, Connie, with Chicago Channel 7 general manager Joe Ahern, at an announcement that the Paytons and their children would serve as grand marshals of a "Say No to Drugs" parade in Chicago. *Courtesy of Chicago Sun-Times, Inc./Photo by Sun-Times Photographer.*

had been picked number one by the Dallas cowboys. He invited some other conference players to a party in Knoxville, Payton among them. The school agreed to pay the athletes' way there, and Hill, a kindly man in the off-season, said to Payton, "Knoxville or New Orleans?" It was no choice. "I liked 'Too Tall' Jones, but I loved Connie Norwood." Payton attended her high school graduation later that year, and she entered Jackson State in the fall. Coincidence or not, Payton's next season was his best as a collegian.

The first game was against the University of Nebraska at Omaha, a strong team. Jackson State won 17–0, and a writer for the Omaha *Daily News* suggested they name the city's Rosenblatt Stadium "Payton Place." (It wasn't the first or last time that obvious play on words had been used.) Payton had 18 carries for 115 yards, caught 5 passes for 72, scored one touchdown, kicked the conversion and a field goal for 10 points. He thought he had one of his least productive games. He might have been frustrated by the muddy field and treacherous footing, but his game would have been considered superior for any other player. The Nebraska coach called him "a tremendous runner. He deserves all the recognition he gets."

"We think of Walter Payton as our Heisman Trophy candidate," Hill said. "It would be great if he could become the first player from a predominantly black school to win the Heisman, but let's face it, we don't have the high-powered publicity the major schools have."

The mid-1970s were an era of racial accommodation. White politicians were aware of the power of new black voters and looked for their support. Mississippi governor William Haller said, "Jackson State is deserving of the full attention and support of all the state officials and people of Mississippi." Lieutenant Governor William Winter visited a team practice and asked to meet Payton. "The potential for good public relations for Mississippi from the Jackson State team," said Winter, "has never been fully realized. We've had a good thing here for years, but only the pro football teams seem to have noticed."

Payton scored only one touchdown in the first four games, but he scored *twenty* in the last seven. Jackson State tied Grambling for the SWAC championship, and Payton's statistics for the season were awesome. In eleven games he had 205 carries for 1,139 yards, a 5.5 average per carry and 103.5 a game. He caught passes for 188 yards and scored 160 points—24 touchdowns, 13 conversions, 1 field goal—to lead the nation.

He was named the SWAC's Most Valuable Player and Offensive Player of the Year, and made the Black All-American team. Payton, always modest, was undergoing a great change in his life. He had always been religious, but now that feeling became central to his life because of his growing success. In Jerry B. Jenkins' book *Sweetness*, published in 1978, Payton said that everything that had happened to him was God's work.

"He was allowing me to be a standout for some reason, and I wanted to know what it was. If it was so that I could point others to Him, then I would always give Him credit. . . . I had had such a rich, full, wonderful life already and I was not even twenty-one years old yet. God had blessed me in ways I could hardly count. There was no way I could take credit for that. God had a purpose for me in all of it."

Jackson State's academic status had been upgraded and the team began the 1974 season as the Jackson State University Tigers. In the fifth game against the University of Nebraska at Omaha, Payton scored six touchdowns. The final game was against Alcorn, undefeated and heading for the conference title, but Payton and his teammates were determined to beat their arch-rival. It was a thrilling game, fought bitterly until the last minute when Jackson State, leading 19–13, stopped the Alcorn fullback two yards from the goal line on fourth down. Payton then carried the ball off-tackle, juking and butting, to give his team breathing room. Then the Jackson State quarterback fell on the ball twice as the seconds ticked off to end the game.

Payton—who is a national spokesman against alcohol abuse—got drunk that night for the first time in his life. He

and a teammate picked up two six-packs of beer to celebrate
the victory. On their way to pick up Connie and another girl,
they started on one can. Then Payton drank five on his own
because the teammate was driving. When he walked in the
door he staggered around, giggling and wobbly, and flopped
on the couch. Connie lectured him, but he heard little of it,
too sick and drunk.

The team had played two fewer games than the year before. Payton carried 175 times for 1,029 yards, a 5.8 average
per carry and 114.3 a game. He set an all-time NCAA record
with 66 touchdowns and 464 total points, and nine Jackson
State records, and all of his records still stand. He was
named College Player of the Year and All-American by many
publications. At that time the NFL draft was held in January, and being voted Most Valuable Offensive Player in the
post-season Senior Bowl and the East-West Shrine game increased Payton's chances to be a number one pick. He had
no particular choice about which team he wanted to draft
him. But he thought he might not get much playing time for
a year or two with a very good team—and liked the idea that
he might make an ordinary team a contender.

Coach Hill wanted to make sure Payton had the right man
to negotiate for him in the draft. He chose Bud Holmes, a
Hattiesburg, Mississippi, lawyer who represented other
players. Payton had a great reputation and was almost certain to be picked in the first round, but he tried to be sensi-
ble about all the draft hullabaloo. Other fine players had
somehow been ignored, and he decided that if he wasn't
drafted he would continue in school. He had finished the
basic B.A. degree requirements in three years and had a
quarter-semester toward his Master's degree in special edu-
cation. He worked hard on his academics, despite the time
and energy consumed by football. He wanted to destroy the

myth that athletes in general, and black athletes in particular, were simply handed a diploma and never learned anything in school.

As expected, he was chosen number one by the Chicago Bears, the fourth pick overall in the draft. He knew little about the Bears except for their most recent heroes, Gale Sayers and Dick Butkus. "About the most excitement I could muster was to wonder what would happen next." All the honors and being a high number one pick seemed almost anticlimactic, but it wasn't false modesty. He loved being recognized as an outstanding player, but that wasn't the reason he played football. He loved the game. He calls it "the purest form of physical combat . . . with something crisp and clean about it, the pure nature of the struggle to play a perfect game."

THE BEARS' MANAGEMENT NOTIFIED PAYTON that they wanted him to meet the Chicago sportswriters at a press conference. He was willing and before he left tried to reach Bud Holmes for advice. When the lawyer was unavailable, he decided to go on his own. At the airport he gave Holmes one more call. They spoke and Holmes said he shouldn't go alone. It wasn't because he thought Payton was too much the small town boy to handle himself in the big city. Always the careful lawyer, Holmes thought it would be better if he went with Payton, but he was trying a case in court and couldn't get away for a few days.

Payton might have gone alone if he had an idea of the furor the delay would cause in Chicago. Bears' officials waited for Payton at O'Hare airport and he didn't show. The writers called all over Mississippi looking for him. They speculated that he either got lost or was just another hick overwhelmed by the idea of Chicago—or, worse, that he was just another spoiled college athlete. Jim Finks, then

General Manager of the Bears, tried to make light of the no-show: "Payton is just a kid from a smaller school with a whole big city focusing attention on him. It can be an awesome thing."

Payton and Holmes reached Chicago three days later. Though far from the big city's idea of a hayseed, Holmes was called "Payton's country lawyer" by sportswriters. Payton was amused and knew it would help in the contract negotiations. Holmes was one of the best known lawyers in Mississippi, a specialist in personal injury cases, legal counsel for the NFL's New Orleans Saints and several professional athletes. "If the Bears or anyone else thought some hick was coming in to try and land me a couple of hundred dollars a week," said Payton, "they were in for a real shock." He insisted on a signing bonus of $126,000 to top Saint's quarterback Archie Manning, who previously received the highest bonus for any NFL player from Mississippi.

Payton was flattered that the Bears, one of the NFL's founding teams, chose him first. They told him that they would have chosen him first of all players in the draft if they had the pick. Gale Sayers, his idol, called to congratulate him. It boosted his morale and he was anxious to get started, but he still wondered if he could make it in the pros. He was confident that his physical ability, skills, and instincts were the equal of any rookie. But when he thought about the big money they were paying him—Chicago was a notoriously closefisted team—and what was expected, he began to have doubts. He understood that almost every man in the pros was "all-everything," too. What if he wasn't fast or tough or big enough? Like an army rookie who is fed stories about the horrors of training, Payton was told of the monstrous playbook and countless formations to learn and "was really scared."

After signing his contract, he and Connie were engaged

but set no wedding date. He wanted to see what would happen in his first year in the pros, whether they would live in Chicago or Mississippi. After graduation he reported to training camp for the college all-star game against the champion Pittsburgh Steelers. His confusion grew. Everyone was saying that he was the next Gale Sayers. Sayers, an exquisite runner, was hailed as probably the greatest who ever played the game. Retired only a few years, he was already a Chicago legend, along with Sid Luckman, Bronko Nagurski, Dick Butkus, Clyde "Bulldog" Turner, George McAfee and owner-coach George Halas. It frightened Payton. He had deep faith in his running ability, but he was no Sayers; their styles couldn't have been more different. It was a lot of pressure for a kid who had never played a minute of pro ball.

In Jerry B. Jenkins' book *Sweetness*, Payton looks back on his first three years in professional football: "I did start faster than Sayers and threatened some of his records and broke others in a shorter playing career—so far. I suppose the comparisons are valid. But back then they were pure speculation and put a lot of pressure on me. And you can't tell me the writers knew I was going to be a record-setting back. That kind of thing starts with every high draft pick. Three months later—when they discover the guy's a bust—he's looking for an assistant coaching job at his old high school and the writers pretend they never predicted anything."

Once training camp for the all-star game began, Payton really felt the pressure. All the other players were getting the same publicity hype, and he was determined to excel in the game. But something else nagged at him. Jack Pardee, then the Bears' coach, said there would be a lot of classroom work in camp. That was no obstacle for Payton. His college coach had emphasized teaching and reviewing film. But he was afraid he'd fall behind by missing the first two weeks of pro camp while with the all-stars.

Competition was fierce in the ex-collegians' camp. Everyone wanted to play and show what he could do against the Steelers (judged by many as the best football team ever). To Payton, however, it was one thing to be chosen one of the country's best college players and another to have his first trial against such an awesome team.

The game was played at Soldier Field, Chicago, on August 1, 1975. To their surprise, the all-stars discovered that even the powerhouse Steelers were vulnerable. They moved 79 yards to the Steeler 28-yard line. California's Steve Bartkowski dropped back to pass. Pittsburgh's strong safety, Mike Wagner, came on a blitz, but Payton leveled him with a lethal block. The pass was completed to Yale's Pat McInally for a touchdown, and Payton's confidence went up a notch.

The Steelers scored early in the second quarter. Then Virgil Livers from Western Kentucky, soon to be a Bear defensive back, ran for a record 88-yard score. At halftime the all-stars led 14–7. Neither team could move the ball in the third quarter. The all-stars struggled to hold their lead and be the first team in more than ten years to beat the pros. But in the last quarter, Joe Gilliam, substituting for Terry Bradshaw, threw two touchdown passes and the all-stars lost 21–14. Payton led his team in rushing, but it was an unimposing 17 yards on 7 carries, and he returned a kickoff 27 yards. It was small consolation to an obsessive overachiever that he was playing against the best defense in football. The next day he was officially a Bear.

Proud, with deep respect for his own ability, Payton asked to go last in the team's speed and strength tests, so he would know the scores he had to beat. Aware of the ill will from his late appearance after the draft, he tried to get off on the right foot with the press, but sportswriters harried him for interviews. Afraid he might say the wrong thing and appear to be a big ego, he became even more close-mouthed than usual. But too often he was casual about appointments with writers and said too little when he did appear. It wasn't because he was rude but because he resented the time taken away from practice or studying the playbook. Stories about him were headlined: PAYTON: SHY GUY WITH FEW WORDS. . . . IS PAYTON WITHDRAWN OR SURLY?

A classic press-athlete war seemed Payton's fate. One writer later spoke of that time. "I think early on he didn't know how to act. He was a small town kid suddenly in the spotlight in a big city. And because he was afraid of presenting the wrong image, he kept on the move and stayed evasive." The misunderstanding with the press lasted only a short time. The writers soon began to see Payton as an endearing but somewhat manic person.

He was careful not to force himself on teammates, but he quickly made friends. He was relaxed around them, and they liked his engaging, mischievous "Peck's Bad Boy" personality. More important, he gained their respect and confidence because of his ability and willingness to work hard. He took on all the tough jobs like blocking that many backs in camp did only grudgingly and rarely to his level. Fullback Roland Harper became his best friend and confidant on the team. Like any smart running back, Payton got close to the offensive linemen, and they taught and encouraged him. They saw a player who might help make the Bears a powerful team again after years in the doldrums.

The all-stars had practiced on artificial turf, and Payton developed an elbow infection from banging his arm too hard and often on the unyielding surface. It got worse in the Bears' camp and caused him severe pain. He didn't want to miss any practice time or pre-season games; he knew how quickly a player, even a first round pick, could get lost. But the infection refused to heal and he tried, with little success, to become resigned to sitting on the bench. It would have frustrated any player trying to impress his coaches, but for someone with Payton's temperament it was torture. He faced missing the first few games after working so hard and worried that he might never fit in with the Bears even after the infection healed. It was bad enough to feel like an outsider by his late start, which he was just overcoming, but now he couldn't play or even practice at full speed.

What impressed him, after all the horror stories about the savage competition in a pro camp, was how helpful his teammates were, even the running backs. It was the first time he understood the feeling of brotherhood, the same bond that exists with all men in a rough, dangerous job. It was the quality that made a good team: the give and take of support, and may the best man win the starting job. Players helped make Payton feel like an integral part of the team by talking to him and teaching him while he was unable to play. Quarterback Bobby Douglass helped the most, going over plays and strategy for hours with the rookie back, doing anything that would help Payton bridge the difficult passage from college to pro running back.

All pro players are affected by the cuts in training camp. They have sympathy for those let go, shrug it off as the order of things, but breathe a little easier until the next cut. Friendships are severed, and there is some guilt when a good player at the same position is let go. Payton was disturbed by the cuts that first training camp, betraying something of the sensitivity that he usually kept hidden. He saw rookies, who thought their dreams and futures were only in football, drift out of camp, along with veterans hoping to hang on for just one more season. Men who were cut usually left quickly, but until they left camp they often became pariahs. Some players still on the roster wouldn't talk to them, as if they would suffer the same fate by the brief contact. Payton, unable then to predict his seemingly endless career, made a touching comment: "I don't know why I'm so sensitive about that. I guess maybe I'll just be sure to quit before it happens to me, because it seems like one of the worst things that can happen to a guy."

The Bears' first preseason opponent was the San Diego Chargers. Ricky Young, Payton's backfield teammate in college, was a Charger draft pick and Payton looked forward to seeing him, but the Bears wanted to get Payton's elbow healed quickly, and he was in a Chicago hospital when the team left for California. He was happy the team won 22–0 but felt terrible about not making the road trip. The next week, still unable to play, Payton watched the Bears lose 13–9 to the Green Bay Packers. He was desperate to play, to contribute, just get into action, but he realized he hadn't even gone through a full-speed hitting workout yet. It was going to be hard to forge his way back as a starter.

During the next week he tried a tough hitting drill, hoping to get himself in shape quickly. Their next opponent was the St. Louis Cardinals and he wanted Coach Pardee to see him perform. But the first time he banged his wrapped elbow on a blocking dummy the pain was agonizing. He had a high pain threshold and thought he could bear it and continue, but it was impossible. He was through for the day and for the game.

The Bears beat the Cardinals 14–13, and their good preseason play made everyone optimistic for the team's prospects. They were a group of young, spirited athletes ready to recapture the Bears' fearsome reputation as "The Monsters of the Midway." Payton hoped to play in the game against the Denver Broncos. He knew Pardee was trying to protect him, not push him too fast, but when the coach told Payton he wouldn't play he was shocked. He had been able to work hard that week and the infection was almost gone. He thought that with the right wrapping and pads he might get in for a couple of series or maybe run back kickoffs. But Pardee stayed firm and Payton watched Chicago lose 13–0 in a rain-soaked game heavy with penalties.

The elbow still hurt, but Payton would let nothing stop him from playing. When he was hit in practice he suffered pain, but he kept his face impassive, even laughing off some hard hits. When the doctor or trainer asked how his elbow felt, he grinned and said, "Perfect." He began to show why he was the Bears' first pick. He exploded through holes, attacked would-be tacklers, and blocked with a bruising intensity. He caught passes and threw the ball on halfback option plays as he faked a run. In every scrimmage he did everything demanded of a great all-around football player.

In those years there were six preseason and fourteen regular season games, so Payton still had a chance to play before the real competition began. Pardee planned to get him into the next game for at least a half. But during the last practice Payton almost blew his chance. Bursting off-tackle, he was banged hard by two tacklers, landed on the bad elbow, and couldn't suppress a grimace. Pardee glanced at the trainer, who shrugged. . . . *Maybe Payton wasn't ready yet.* But he would not be kept out of a fifth straight game. He made his professional debut against the Dolphins in Miami's Orange Bowl on a hot, humid night in early September.

A Dolphin defensive back intercepted Bobby Douglass's first pass and returned it 54 yards for a score. The Bears were sluggish and Miami won 21–10. Payton was supposed to play only the first half. He gained 60 yards on 12 carries against Miami's fine defense, and Pardee, excited by his prize rookie, let him play the third quarter. The Miami defense began keying on him and gang-tackled—as would happen to him for years when he was the Bears' only offensive threat—and he gained only 8 more yards on 7 carries. He was disappointed he didn't do better in the second half but he still gained more yardage than any Chicago back during the exhibition season and he felt better after seeing his first game action.

His mother came up from Columbia to stay with him for a while. Her presence, her cooking, and her uncommon good sense helped his transition to the pro game. They were a mother and son who truly enjoyed each other, laughed together. He often came home muttering about coaches who yelled at him in practice, and his mother would remind him of his relationship with Eddie. He always resented his older brother's attempts to teach him how to run the ball, how to catch and carry it, and he always stormed out of the house. He quickly got the point and returned to practice the next day eager to learn. His mother, he said, "always had a way of bringing me down to earth. She never bossed me around, just encouraged me with the right word or example. Mostly it was just inspiring to have her there. She made the good games better and the bad games easier to take."

7

THE BEARS OPENED THE 1975 REGULAR SEASON at home against the Baltimore Colts. Like Chicago, the Colts were once a powerhouse and were rebuilding. The Bears were a 2-point favorite, but the Colts whipped them 35–7. Payton's pro debut was a disaster. He gained zero yards in his first 8 carries and lost 2 yards on 4 pass receptions. To make the loss more distasteful, the sewers backed up in the Bears' locker room before the game. One sportswriter suggested that they had brought the foul smell onto the field with them. Payton was depressed after the loss and his performance. He was afraid he had lost the chance to start again, but Pardee reassured him that he was the Bears' halfback.

The next game against the Philadelphia Eagles was a tough, tight battle. Late in the fourth quarter, the Eagles led 13–12. Chicago had the ball on its own 37-yard line—3rd down and 14 yards to go. The Bears knew it would be their last chance to score. Payton had committed two 15-yard

Taking a handoff from the quarterback. *Courtesy of Chicago Bears.*

penalties and put the team in a hole, the first for a late hit, the second for clipping (blocking a man from behind). Like any fierce competitor, he thought the penalties were unfair and wanted the ball to redeem himself. The Eagles' defense dropped back to protect against a long pass, conceding the short-gainer.

Quarterback Gary Huff hit Payton for 11 yards to the 48-yard line. The Bears had to go on 4th down—3 yards for a first down. Huff took a quick drop and threw to Payton again. The pass was low, but Payton slid his hands under the ball like a scoop and pulled it in before it hit the ground. It was a first down, but they had to get much closer for a field goal try. Huff threw a swing pass to Payton. An Eagle line-backer grabbed his jersey, but he pulled away and bulled downfield for another 11 yards to the Eagle 37. An off-tackle play was stopped for no gain. The Eagles expected a pass, but Huff crossed them up and sent Payton up the middle, the most basic play in football. An Eagle lineman had him stopped just beyond the line of scrimmage, but he spun out of the tackle and behind good downfield blocking ran 24 yards to the Eagle 13. Two plays later, with eight seconds left on the clock, Bob Thomas kicked the field goal for a 15–13 Bears' victory.

Payton had his first good game as a pro, 21 carries for 95 yards, 6 receptions for 36—but was modest in the postgame interviews. He said that if Huff had gone to fullback Cid Edwards or a wide receiver the result would have been the same. Possibly, but in that game Payton showed that he was the ultimate clutch player, the man who can produce under pressure in situations that spell victory or defeat.

A veteran football observer said he didn't believe other players could have done what Payton did: "Don't you believe it. Sure, it's possible, they're pros. But there is always just one guy you can trust with the ball when the going is really tough. The one guy who can get you the yards to win. Payton may be only a rookie, but I predict he's going to be a pressure guy. There are runners who look like comets in practice. Get them in a game and they can't really move the ball. If they were with Moses at the parting of the Red Sea, they would have been only halfway across before the hole closed. Players like Payton *get there*! He'd be on the opposite shore waiting to hand the ball to Moses so he could spike it."

The Minnesota Vikings were the first Central Division opponent the Bears faced. The Vikings, a powerful team, beat them 28–3 in Minneapolis but didn't dominate the Bears, despite the score. Payton looked forward to playing them in Chicago in a few weeks. He thought they could be beaten. In pro ball as well as college, he realized, it was foolish to fear a team because of its reputation. The game, as the cliché goes, is played on the field. He had run for a respectable 61 yards and, more important, noted that the Vikings' fierce front four, Carl Eller, Jim Marshall, Alan Page, Gary Larsen—the "Purple People Eaters"—hadn't stomped or crushed him.

The next two games were losses to Detroit (27–7) and Pittsburgh (34–3). The Bears had a record of 1–4, had scored only three touchdowns, and were outscored 137 to 35. They were to face the Vikings the next week and suddenly Payton wasn't that sure the Bears could beat them. He was depressed again after being held to no gain in 10 carries against Detroit and suffering a bruised knee in the Pittsburgh game. Mike Adamle replaced him in the Pittsburgh game and rushed for 110 yards on 10 carries, the best game by a Bear running back since Gale Sayers. Fullback Roland Harper gained 86, for a team total of 196 yards on the ground. It was a superior effort against the best team in football. Hope ran high for the return against Minnesota.

The Bears played the Vikings in Soldier Field on a Monday night. Their defense stiffened and they held their opponent to just 13 points, but they couldn't capitalize on a number of scoring chances. Adamle scored on a 14-yard draw play for 7–0 Chicago lead. Later in the game, leading 7–3, the Bears had the ball on the Vikings' 6-yard line, but Payton fumbled it away. The game was lost 13–9. Payton gained 44 yards on 10 carries. He hadn't scored a touchdown yet that season, and his few bright spots were in the Philadelphia game and on some long kickoff returns.

The Miami Dolphins beat them 46–13, the most points against a Chicago team in three years, and their 1–6 start was the worst Chicago record since 1969. Payton scored his first touchdown in that game, but as he later said, "At that point, the best thing about professional football was the money." As hard as he played, he couldn't help being disappointed. Any athlete accustomed to winning and dominating suffers in defeat. For a passionate competitor like Payton it was hell. He blamed himself for some of the losses. To make matters worse, Adamle, a small, stocky, darting back, was running so well he started instead of Payton.

The second half of the season began on a slightly brighter note when the Bears beat the Green Bay Packers 27–14. But it was nearly a disaster for Payton. Adamle piled up yardage while Payton ran the wrong way on two plays, and, according to one writer, forced Gary Huff "to run for his life." His one bright spot in the game was a patented five-yard butting, struggling run into the end zone carrying a Packer safety on his back. There were three more road defeats after that victory: 31–3 to the San Francisco Forty-Niners, 38–10 to the Los Angeles Rams, 28–7 to the Packers. Payton's first

100-yard game as a pro (105 yards) against San Francisco was small comfort. In the Rams game he didn't play until the second half after bruising his leg on the opening kickoff. He gained 2 yards on 4 carries "and might as well have stayed home." The game against the Packers in Green Bay was played in a driving snowstorm, the wind chill well below zero. The Packers led 28–0 at the half, but the Bears saved some face by holding them scoreless the rest of the game and scoring a touchdown.

The Bears split the next two games at home, beating Detroit 25–21 and losing 34–20 to a fast St. Louis Cardinal team. Pardee started three rookies in the backfield against Detroit: quarterback Bob Avellini, Payton, and Harper. Payton scored twice and gained 65 yards on 27 carries (his most as a pro). The Cardinals, who went on to win the Eastern Division title, humiliated the Bears until the fourth quarter when the Bears scored all twenty of their points. Payton scored once, ran for 58 yards on 17 carries, and caught 4 passes for 37 yards.

The season's last game was against the New Orleans Saints. A day before the game, Payton was disturbed by a football writer's column that said Payton had played like the rookie he was in the first thirteen games. It implied that he was something of a disappointment. He agreed he hadn't played nearly as well as he hoped and was determined to show what he could do—and in that game he came into his own.

He carried the ball 25 times for 134 yards (including a 54-yard touchdown), caught 5 passes for 62 yards, and returned 2 kickoffs for 104 yards. One 69-yard return was a perilous, slithering jaunt through enemy players. He was twice hemmed in on the sideline and escaped by reversing his field. He had 300 total yards, about as much as an entire team gains on a decent day. Despite his slow start, losing playing time to Adamle, and the team's poor record, Payton's first-year statistics were impressive:

196 carries for 679 yards, a 3.5 average per carry, and 7 touchdowns.

14 kickoff returns for 444 yards, a 31.7 average, which made him the NFL kickoff return leader for the year.

33 pass receptions for 213 yards, a 6.5 average.

1 punt return for 39 yards.

He was disappointed in his 679 yards rushing, but it made him the most productive Bears runner since Gale Sayers gained 1,032 in 1969. He ranked third in the National Football Conference (the league has two conferences: National and American) and ninth overall in the NFL in rushing. There were expert observers who granted that Payton had a good year and showed versatility, but they expected more from a number one pick.

On the way home to Columbia he stopped in Jackson to visit his old school. He felt a curious alienation as he walked around the campus. Athletes he'd played with and students who were in his classes were still there, but he felt awkward because they treated him like a professional football player, a celebrity. He wanted to be part of that safe, warm, insulated life just a little longer, but he understood that it was gone forever for him.

Payton, Ricky Young, and other Jackson State players in the pros worked out together to keep in shape. They ran the sandbank and levees, played basketball, and improvised games to keep their reflexes sharp. Payton quickly discovered what being a member of the Chicago Bears meant, how professional athletes were idolized in America. Before, when he had spoken to various groups, "people wondered who this Walter Payton was and where was this Jackson

77

State University. Now I was *Walter Payton—Chicago Bears.* I had instant credibility. I was somebody. I was a pro. I was from the National Football League."

He hadn't set the league on fire, was no instant star, and had only completed a rookie year that promised great things in the future. But he found himself lionized, asked for autographs, met movie stars and politicians. A little confused by the attention, he insisted that he was "still just Walter. I wasn't special." But he was. Perhaps not for what he did that first year, but, like all great young athletes, for his physical elegance that raised him above the ordinary.

Sports are ingrained in American life, a means of relieving the boredom and anxiety of the everyday, an outlet for strong emotions. Watching an athlete at the peak of his youth and skills is to see the extraordinary made to look ordinary. But in our hearts we know better, and have great respect for the athlete's craft. The silliest phrase is the sportscaster's "Grown men playing a little boy's game." What we did bumblingly as children and adolescents—with perhaps an occasional flash of physical genius—we watch athletes do with regularity and excellence.

The great athlete practices his or her craft at a very high level, without fakery—no small thing when in many areas of life today fraud and fakery are almost commonplace. The superior athlete's performance of a sport is fraud-free and fakeproof. A running back weaving through a mass of tacklers on a kickoff, beset everywhere by danger, making the precise, instinctive move that springs him free . . . the boxer throwing the hook that leaves him vulnerable . . . a pitcher shaving the plate with a curve on a 3–2 count and the bases full . . . the daredevil racing driver taking a curve flat out— all are beyond public relations, endorsements, drug scandals, or contract squabbles.

78

Payton couldn't be expected to understand what he was beginning to mean to people. He enjoyed the attention and gave freely of his time. He rationalized it as giving happiness to others. In *Sweetness* he talked about those first days of adulation:

"I know people get a kick out of meeting me or any professional athlete. If I'm able to bring them any kind of enjoyment by shaking their hand or talking with them, I'm happy to do it. It's one of the things God put me on earth for—to make people happy and to enjoy life. If it makes them feel good, it makes me feel good, too." Then he made a statement he may have reconsidered later when the attention got out of hand. "But I want people to be able to go further. I want them to be able to relate to me."

But he wanted no such thing. A private person, he began to dislike the fan and media attention that took away time he wanted to spend with his wife. Later, when they had children, it would get worse. At first, he never put off anyone who wanted to talk with him, but as his fame grew he found it more difficult. In his second year, when he began to be a team leader and led the league in rushing, he knew that his life had changed forever. His time would never be his own again.

He looked forward to the 1976 season. He worked hard conditioning himself for what he hoped would be a banner year. Most importantly, he and Connie had been married July 7. He was "totally happy with myself for the first time in my life." He knew Connie would be a settling presence in Chicago during the season. He was more confident after that first year, felt like a veteran, and knew the Bears planned to use him more.

In training camp, despite the team's poor 1975 season, Payton found no discord. He admired Jack Pardee for the way he kept the club together, without the backbiting and turmoil that goes with losing. Players were spirited and encouraged each other. As in every training camp in the league, there was an air of optimism. The Bears were still a young team but now not quite so green.

Payton's only problem was driving himself too hard. Because he had a promising rookie year and knew everyone expected more of him, he thought he had to carry the team. He couldn't relax and began to experience nausea and headaches and dizziness. The doctors told him he was too intense, subconsciously driving himself too hard, taking on too much responsibility for the team's success. It was taking a terrible toll on his nerves. Worse, Payton knew, it was affecting his play. He was too tight. He realized that he could only do his best, play at the top of his skills, and let the rest take care of itself. It was a valuable lesson that led to his almost-epic career.

He would simply go out and give everything of himself. What was going to happen would happen. It wasn't for him to worry about; otherwise, he'd drive himself crazy thinking about it. Like other splendid runners, Payton knew he ran out of fear—not the fear of injury but the fear of what a runner can't predict. One play he runs easily for a long gain; the next he's mauled by tacklers and thrown to the ground under flying bodies, the body taking shock after shock. He learned not to think that he had to score a touchdown every time he carried the ball. His sights would always be set on the end zone. But when a play was over, even if no-gain or an advance of 2 yards by brute struggle, it was over. Get back to the huddle, line up for the play, and give it another shot.

THE 1976 PRESEASON OPENED AGAINST THE BRONCOS in
Denver's Mile High Stadium. Payton suffered a knee strain
and had only a few carries in Chicago's win. He sat out
the victory over the Seattle Seahawks but was ready for the
(then) Baltimore Colts. Pardee told him he might carry the
ball as much as 30 times because he needed game action. He
was like a thoroughbred too long in the stable and now
turned loose. Playing before a sellout crowd at home, Payton
had a superb game: 31 carries for 122 yards, 3 catches for 24
yards in a convincing win. He had good games against the
St. Louis Cardinals and Tampa Bay Bucs but was kept out of
the Washington Redskins game to make sure his knee would
be strong for the regular season.

The Bears were 5–1 in exhibition play, and though it
wasn't always an indication of a team's real ability, the early
feeling of confidence seemed justified. In the season opener
they beat Detroit in a dull, frustrating game. The next week

against the Forty-Niners in Candlestick Park in San Francisco, Payton had his best game as a pro. A writer thought he might have been inspired by Gale Sayers's miracle game in 1965 against the same team in the same park. In one of the greatest individual performances in football history, Sayers ran for six touchdowns, an NFL record he shares with only one player, Ernie Nevers of the old Chicago Cardinals who did it in 1929. Payton ran for two touchdowns and gained 148 yards on 28 carries. It was the biggest day for a Chicago back since Sayers's club record of 205 against the Packers in 1968.

Brimming with confidence, the Bears poured onto the field to play the winless Atlanta Falcons. They wanted to be the first Bears' team to start the season with three wins since 1963, a championship year. But the strong Falcons' defense held them scoreless and they lost 10–0. Still, there was no feeling among the Bears that they would repeat the disastrous season of the preceding year. The team came into Washington and beat the Redskins 33–7. It was to become characteristic of the entire season—whipping an undefeated team after losing to a winless one. Jack Pardee talked to his players after the game and gave a good evaluation of the Bears that year. "We have to do everything right because we're not a real good team and we're not a real bad team." Payton gained 104 yards against the Redskins for his second 100-yard game of the year. Four games into the schedule, he led the NFL with 408 yards and a 4.3 average per carry.

The Bears didn't play to their ability on the road against the Vikings, Rams, and Cowboys, and the encouraging 3–1 record went to 3–4. Payton, always the team man, got little satisfaction out of his 2 touchdowns and 141 yards on only 19 carries against the Vikings for a 7.3 average. Or his 145 yards on 27 carries against the Rams. He was injured early in the

Cowboys' game and gained just 41 yards. He and the other players were disturbed because they had been competitive in all three losing games. If they had done this, or changed that, or avoided mistakes, they would be leading the league.

In their first home game in almost a month, they beat the Vikings 14–13 despite being heavily outgained. Back to .500, there again was talk of a successful season. Payton rode the roller coaster of emotion, as optimistic as the others, but "in the next game we suffered our most bitter loss of the season." They faced one of the league's dominant teams, the (then) Oakland Raiders. Some players didn't honestly think they could compete with the Raiders but never voiced their doubts. The majority of the Bears knew they were capable of very good play and went out to win. "It was a nightmare," recalled Payton. He was less than 100 percent physically; his ankle was tender, but like many pesky injuries, it hurt less when he was running.

The Bears took a first-quarter lead on Payton's 5-yard touchdown run. The Raiders tied the score in the second quarter on a pass from Ken Stabler to tight end Dave Casper. Later in the period the Raiders took the lead on a 75-yard bomb from Stabler to Cliff Branch. They added another touchdown in the third quarter and led 21–7. But the Bears didn't fold, showing that indefinable element of the game usually called "character." Bob Avellini threw 36 yards to wide receiver Bo Rather for a touchdown. Payton then scored two touchdowns within three minutes. An extra point was missed, but the Bears were ahead 27–21. It promised to be the upset of the year.

The surprises continued. A Stabler fumble was run in for a score by tackle Roger Stillwell and the Bears led 33–21. But the referee had blown the play dead when he saw the ball squirt loose and the confused Raiders never pursued Stillwell. The referee later admitted he had made a mistake. The Bears' defense tried desperately to hold the slim lead, but Stabler threw 49 yards to Branch for a touchdown. The play was another indication of the Bears' bad luck in the game. Virgil Livers, the defensive back covering Branch, played the receiver perfectly and knocked the ball away—right into Branch's hands. Trailing 28–27, Chicago had a last chance. With only 20 seconds to play, Bob Thomas tried a 21-yard field goal. He hit it true and the Bears began jumping in victory. But a fickle, swirling wind took the ball right and it hit the upright and bounced back on the field.

Despite his bad ankle, Payton had a fine game. He scored 3 touchdowns, ran 97 yards on 37 carries, the latter a club record. For the season he had 11 touchdowns and was 1 yard short of 1,000 in just nine games. Writers predicted he'd break Sayers's record of 1,231 yards. "To me, it was all hollow at that point." He knew the Bears were a better team than their 4–5 record, and it ate at him that he might not be performing at his best, despite what the experts said. Friends, who should have known better, said he should at least be happy with his excellent season. His reply: "When I become satisfied with a great day, I'd better quit."

Off the field he was still the irrepressible kid despite another disappointing season. Without his intense, aggressive game face, he had the look and smile of a choir boy. While other players conserved their energy as much as possible between games, Payton couldn't sit still. He danced, he drummed, he drove cars fast, and couldn't run the most ordinary errand for his wife without stopping at a golf driving range. Energy leaked from every pore. "I was born that way," he said, "having to move."

"He's a man-child, a grown-up kid," said safety Gary Fencik. "He's always out there throwing and kicking and shooting his bow and arrow and a dozen other things. I've never known anyone who likes to play outdoors so much. It's not even football. I used to worry that he'd get hurt. I used to pray every night. But he's got a frame that just seems invincible."

Payton loved the horseplay in the locker room, a cutup who was a prime practical joker. He snapped towels, lit firecrackers, and during a meeting when everyone was half-asleep he'd let out a piercing scream just for the hell of it. Once he was in an assistant coach's office when a firecracker suddenly went off in the locker room. Everyone ran around, yelling "Walter! Where's Walter?" Payton said, "Coach, I've been sitting with you, so you know it wasn't me, but I'm going to be blamed for this." Later he was asked if he might have used a delayed fuse. Gosh, he replied, he was just a country boy and didn't know about things like that. Then he grinned. "Well, maybe we did some of that in high school and college. Tape a cigarette to an M-80 or a cherry bomb, stick it somewhere and light the cigarette."

In the tenth game of the season the Bears beat Green Bay to even their record at 5–5. Payton ran for 109 yards to become the first Chicago back since Sayers to break 1,000 in a season. There were constant comparisons between the two, and Payton fought the identification with a Bears' legend, a player who was already an NFL immortal:

"It's unfair to compare me to Sayers. I've played less than two years while he had seven great seasons. I brought my own history and style and personality to the Bears. It honors me to be mentioned in the same breath with him, but I think it's a bit of an insult to him. If the writers want to say I'm being falsely modest, let them."

He presented each offensive lineman with a gold watch, inscribed on the back with a simple but eloquent tribute:

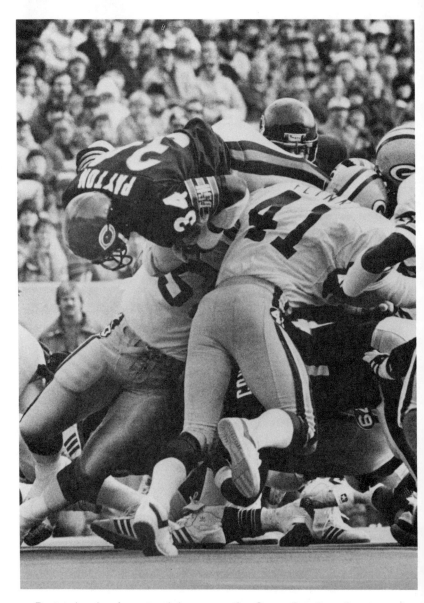

Payton leaping for a touchdown over the Green Bay line. *Courtesy of Chicago Sun-Times, Inc./Photo by Sun-Times Photographer.*

Thanks for the 1,000 yards. Other great runners rewarded their blockers, but Payton did something more; he gave his linemen self-esteem and helped them play to the utmost of their ability. Jackie Slater, a Ram offensive tackle who blocked for Payton at Jackson State, said linemen are affected by a runner with Payton's ability and personality:

"A lot of times in college I'd do half my job and Walter would break a long run anyway. Then he'd tell the press it was my block that sprung him loose, when all the time I knew the block could have been a whole lot better. That kind of thing builds. You start to get confidence in yourself. Now the lineman say to themselves, 'Hey, we've got an all-pro back there—we've got to block all-pro to keep him going.'"

In the next to last game of the 1976 season, Payton had his best day as a Bear. If that sounds repetitious, it would continue throughout his career, a measure of the goals he set for himself, the perfection he was constantly seeking. The Bears demolished the Seahawks 34–7 and Payton gained 183 yards, just 22 yards short of Sayers's single game record of 205 yards. But he had the satisfaction of breaking Sayers's season record in that game. He also led O. J. Simpson by 9 yards in the race for the NFL rushing crown.

The final game was against the Broncos in Soldier Field. The sports pages and television were filled with the Payton-Simpson race. The team, however, was concerned with finishing at 8–6 for the best Bears' record in years. Coach Pardee was tired of answering questions about risking injury for Payton by running him so much. That season, Payton's fanatical assaults on the defense cost him enormous amounts of energy. There were times when he would so totally exhaust himself he had to suck oxygen on the sideline before he could return to the game.

One writer claimed that Payton had been sent in for three quick plays at the end of the Seahawk game because team officials heard that Simpson was ahead by a few yards. But the same thing was said about Simpson. The charges were groundless. In those days the Bears were among the poorest passing teams, and their offense was to run Payton again and again and again. "I was being paid to run the ball," he said. There was an interesting sidelight to Pardee's appreciation of Payton. An ex-linebacker for the Rams and Redskins, Pardee was one of the toughest players of his era. He so admired Payton's tackling that sometimes players on the sideline got the idea he looked forward to interceptions against his own team so he could see Payton reverse roles and pound someone.

He gained only 49 yards and a touchdown against the Broncos before suffering a bad ankle sprain early in the third quarter. The game was lost 28–14, but Payton also lost the chance to beat out Simpson for the NFL rushing title. It was almost O. J.'s last hurrah as he beat out Payton, the heir apparent. Payton was crushed, but he said he never wanted the title for himself alone but for his linemen. When he was taken out of the game, he covered his face and cried from the disappointment, the fatigue, and the aftereffects of a crushing hit on his last play—but mostly from the letdown, knowing that the season was over. Fans were startled; they had never seen anything like that before. His teammates were shocked but sympathetic as they watched the usually stoic Payton in tears. One by one they came to the bench where he sat, head in hands, and gave him silent encouragement with a touch or pat. So many things had come together at that moment, he tried to explain later, he was just overwhelmed.

Payton quickly recovered and took some pride in what

he'd accomplished in his second season. Fans and writers always added "and with a lousy team," but he never blamed anyone that he hadn't done better. He finished with 1,390 yards on 311 carries for a 4.5 average. He was named *Sporting News* Player of the Year and runner-up to Chuck Foreman of the Vikings for NFC Most Valuable Offensive Player. He led the league in rushing and broke the Bears' season rushing record. He received 39 out of a possible 42 votes for the United Press International All-NFC squad and was named to the NFL all-pro backfield with Simpson by the Associated Press. He ran his total of 100-yard-plus games to 9, moved into ninth place in Bears rushing history, and picked up his fourth and fifth game balls for the Forty-Niners and Packers games.

Payton was well liked by his teammates, but writers still found him difficult on occasion. He wasn't antagonistic, just uninterested; writers didn't help him win. During an interview he might open his mail or begin to walk to his car, letting the writer trail after him. It may account for the relatively little publicity he received until his records were so overwhelming he had become a national sports hero. During the off-season, writers badgered him, asking if he thought he could beat out O. J. Simpson for the rushing title. He always said yes, an unusual response for a professional athlete. The question was usually answered by modest disclaimers, compliments for his rival, speculations about the injury factor and fate, and earnestness about simply doing one's best. But Payton wasn't boasting. He truly believed he could do it in the coming season.

Before training camp he again went through his grueling conditioning program. Though only in his third pro year, he wanted to test himself on the hill against younger college players. "My goal was to make them drop. That hill's angle is about 45 degrees in a 50-foot rise. Ever jog up twenty-five flights of stairs? It burns. Your legs, your buttocks, your back, your chest, your stomach—everything wants to leave you." Struggling up and down the hill in early summer heat, the college athletes soon quit. Payton looked at them and then ran the hill one last time, like a coup de grace, the killing shot. He decided that his medium-sized hands weren't strong enough and worked on them until they became like bear traps.

That same off-season, Don Pierson of the *Chicago Tribune*, a writer Payton liked, visited him in Jackson, where the family had recently moved from nearby Columbus.

"It was the most frantic eleven hours I've ever spent," said Pierson. "Walter picked me up at the airport. He had a CB radio in his car and his handle was Mississippi Maniac. All I could think of was, 'Thank God for his reflexes,' because we were going seventy-five all over the road. It was hot as blazes and he had the radio on and he sang while we talked. When we got to his house, he turned on the stereo and the TV and started folding laundry.

"Then he went into his den and started playing the drums to the stereo, and I remember he said, 'This is like doing seventy pushups.' After that he and five buddies ran up and down the banks of the Pearl River till they were exhausted, after which we drove to a brewery for beer. When we got back to his house, Walter got a hose and started watering the lawn.

"After that he went inside and simultaneously played chess with a friend and watched TV. He was standing and slapping his thighs, saying, 'Move! Move! I can't stand it when you play slow.' He then dragged me off to buy some stereo equipment before heading to a driving range to hit golf balls. We met Connie, ate dinner in fifteen minutes, and Walter drove me to the airport to catch a plane. While we waited in the concourse Walter acted as if he was holding a bowling ball and making throwing motions. I'll never forget that. He'd done almost every sport that day and now he was bowling down the hallway. I asked him if he ever slept and he said, 'Yeah, I sleep. You don't think I sleep? You think this is twenty-four hours nonstop?'"

IT WAS A DIFFERENT PAYTON who reported to the Bears' training camp for the 1977 season. He was in glowing good health, his spirits were high, and he had no injuries or fears, no mental exhaustion or nervousness. Again, he was optimistic about the Bears' chances. The Vikings, perennial Central Division winners, were an aging team. The coaches worked him hard, but he didn't carry the ball much in the exhibition season except in the Cleveland game, when he had a chance to compete against his brother Eddie for the first time. He was being protected, saved for the games that counted. The day of the opener against Detroit he was ready to run, but he could hardly have predicted the remarkable season he'd have.

In the Bears' 30–20 win over Detroit, Payton ran for 160 yards on 23 carries and scored two touchdowns. In the second quarter he had the longest run of his career, 73 yards to set up another touchdown. But the writers called him the goat in the next game against St. Louis. Trailing 16–13 with 19 seconds to play, Payton shot off-tackle, trying to gain enough yards to make a last-ditch field goal possible, but time ran out on the Bears. He was criticized for not running out of bounds to stop the clock, but he said he tried and had no excuses. "I tried to juke one guy and move outside, but another forced me inside and I couldn't adjust quick enough."

He had three touchdowns against New Orleans, but the Bears lost 42–24. He had one long run of 49 yards and gained 140 yards on 19 carries. But, again, he couldn't be happy with his fine game. It was the best Bears team he had played on, and once more the start of the season just promised more of the disappointment that had marked his first two years.

There was a poignant moment in pro football history in a Monday night game against the Los Angeles Rams. Joe Namath, formerly a New York Jets' star, was the Rams' quarterback and one of the game's greatest passers, making a last attempt to hold on. Harassed and battered by the Chicago pass rush, Namath played poorly. He completed only 16 of 40 passes, was knocked out of the game, and was soon cut by the Rams. In the Bears' 24–23 victory, Payton, the new great, ran for 126 yards in 24 carries. It was the end of one era, the beginning of another.

There was one sour moment for Payton in the game. Isaiah Robinson, a Ram linebacker, threatened him for clipping safety Bill Simpson. Payton dismissed it as something said in the heat of a game, but Robinson told the press he'd end Payton's career if he ever got the chance. Payton was distraught when he read the story and talked about it in *Sweetness:*

"I believed Robinson and it shook me. I would never intentionally hurt another ballplayer. I've clipped before, and I may have in this case, but it has never been intentional. I'm an aggressive player who reacts on instinct. I play hard and fast and I can make mistakes or get turned around. A play can switch directions. You can shoot at someone and have them turn at the last moment. Football is a dangerous game, but I play it straight and clean. And I hope by my reputation alone that Isaiah Robinson knows that by now. Even if he doesn't, I do, and that's what counts."

Next was a loss to Minnesota, the archrival. Then a loss to the Atlanta Falcons. The Bears were beating themselves, losing games they should have won, and it was frustrating to Payton and his teammates:

"It isn't so bad when you know you don't have a winning team and you just go out and do your best. You take every win you can, but you look for other things to encourage you—a better day on defense, a good kicking game, whatever. But we were past that. We weren't looking for that kind of encouragement. We were a team that should have been winning and that's what we wanted."

They whipped the Packers 26–0 at Green Bay, and Payton could finally savor a great day. He tied Sayers's single-game Bears' record of 205 yards on 23 carries, a sterling 8.9 average per carry. He told Pardee he'd like one more carry to break the record, but the coach said no, despite the eleven minutes left on the clock. Green Bay was beaten and there was no reason to risk injury to Payton. It was a day the team played to its ability and Payton felt he "could do anything." Breaking tackles with ease and accelerating with jet bursts of speed, he seemed almost too dominant for any team to stop.

But there was criticism from the purists who couldn't accept Payton's unorthodox, slam-bang, flailing style of running. Some defenders thought he should just fall when he was hit. But he had been taught—and it was his nature—to scratch and fight and dig for every yard, "every extra inch I can weasel out of a play." Some observers said he ran that way because he didn't plan to play too many years anyway. No back could survive for long fighting and clawing that way on every play. Payton said it was the only way he knew how to run.

He led the league in rushing by a good margin but was saddened when he heard that O. J. Simpson had undergone knee surgery less than halfway through the season. He wanted to go head to head with Simpson. To him Simpson was one of the three greatest runners, along with Sayers and Jim Brown. He sensed it was the end of O. J.'s career. A young player might survive a knee injury, but for a veteran running back who had run miles with a football and taken too many hard hits, it was almost certainly the end.

In their eighth game the Bears suffered a humiliating 47–0 loss to the Houston Oilers. Their record stood at 3 wins and 5 losses. The next game was at home against the Kansas City Chiefs. It would be the wildest, most dramatic battle of the year, decided by a point.

The Bears fell behind 17–0 in the first half and the fans booed them mercilessly. They fought back, with Payton running up big yardage. He scored two touchdowns; then, with 2:02 to play, he scored a third to put Chicago on top 21–20. But there was little time to celebrate. The Chiefs had a long return on the kickoff after Payton's touchdown. Then Ed Podolak swept the end for a 27–21 lead. The Soldier Field crowd began to leave. The Bears took the kickoff and moved quickly to the Chiefs' 37-yard line. The clock was running down as Bob Avellini dropped back for a last desperate pass. He saw the Chiefs' strong safety hesitate in covering tight end Greg Latta and threw the ball. It was to Latta's wrong side, but he whirled and made a stunning catch for a touchdown and a 28–27 Chicago win. Payton, with 79 yards on 20 carries, went over the 1,000-yard mark for the second straight year. At 4–5, the Bears thought there was still a chance for the playoffs if they won their remaining five games.

The next week Payton came down with the flu and many players were injured or badly bruised. They had to face the Vikings, leading the Division at 6–3. The Vikings, like all teams, prepared by watching film of their opponent's most recent games. Whenever Payton ran, they burst into spontaneous applause, the ultimate tribute of solid professionals. Before the game, defensive end Carl Eller passed Payton on the field and said, "You're the greatest running back I've ever seen." He could hardly imagine what he'd see that day.

On game day Payton still felt weak and his body ached. Many athletes often surpass themselves when suffering illness or injury. Payton did nothing less than have the greatest single game of any running back in NFL history.

Forty times Payton was handed the ball and he slammed into the Minnesota defenders behind a battered line playing with great dedication. He gained a single-game record 275 yards for a 10–7 win. After the game writers asked him how he did it with a bad case of flu. "If the game had gone into overtime," Payton said casually, "I imagine I could have gone some more." The ultimate perfectionist, he managed to find several plays where he should have gained more yardage. With the 275-yard game, Payton began his first serious assault on the rushing records. He:

• Broke Simpson's single game standard of 273 yards, set only the year before.

• Broke the club record of 205 yards he shared with Sayers.

• Broke his own record of 36 carries.

• Ran for over 100 yards for the sixteenth time in his career and tied Rick Casares for the club record of seven 100-yard games in a season.

• Broke his Bears' season record of 1,390 yards with 1,404.

• Ran for 200 yards for the second time in his career.

He now had 1,404 in 10 games. When Simpson set his season record of 2,003 yards in 1973, he had just 1,323 in 10 games. Payton was 81 yards ahead of his pace, but Simpson had closed with back-to-back 200-yard games. Payton figured he needed an average of 150 yards per game to beat Simpson by a yard.

Preparing for the Thanksgiving game against Detroit, Payton was swarmed by the media after his brilliant game—"as if I had just been discovered." He was interviewed by seventeen reporters on a nationwide hookup. The Professional Football Hall of Fame at Canton, Ohio, called and asked for his jersey. He hated the distractions, especially during a short practice week, but cooperated.

Eddie had been traded to Detroit from Cleveland, and the brothers played against each other in a regular league game for the first time. Payton gained 136 yards on 20 carries, and the Bears went to 6–5 with a 31–14 victory. The weak Tampa Bay Bucs held them scoreless until the fourth quarter when they eked out a 10–0 win, but Payton gained only 101 yards on 33 carries. If his shot at Simpson's record now seemed slim, the Bears—7–5 with two games to go—still had a chance for the playoffs. They beat Green Bay 21–10 and Payton rushed 32 times for 163 yards.

He trailed Simpson by 198 yards, needed 199 to beat him in the last game. His offensive linemen wanted it for him as badly as Simpson's linemen had four years before. Chicago and Minnesota were tied for the Division lead at 8–5. Playing on Saturday, the Vikings clinched the top spot. The Bears were still confident. They had won five straight and felt they were among the league's better teams. Payton wanted the record, but he wanted a victory over the New York Giants more. It would ensure the Bears a place in the playoffs for the first time since 1963.

Game day in Giant Stadium broke in a cold heavy rain. The Bears weren't too concerned; the field had good drainage, and footing on the artificial turf wasn't affected too badly. But the rain turned to hail and sleet, making the stadium turf as glassy as a skating rink. By the opening kickoff, the field was covered with ice and slush, and it would get worse during the game. Teammates looked at Payton and thought he'd be terribly disappointed, but he had already "conceded the record to the weather and wasn't going to whimper about it." He was rousing everyone to have a great game, slapping players on the back, butting helmets, grinning, kidding around. Winning seemed the only thing on his mind.

The Giants had a poor team that year, but that made them all the more dangerous. They concentrated on having that one big game that might salvage something from the season. At halftime the game was tied 3–3. Payton had worn rubber-soled sneakers in the first half but couldn't get any traction. He concentrated on holding on to the ball. During the game the field had become even icier and harder under the slush and water, and he changed into regular artificial turf shoes. It helped only a little in the treacherous footing.

Payton had a miserable day running. He carried the ball only 15 times for 47 yards. When Pardee saw how well Larry Csonka, the big Giant fullback, was doing, he ran his own fullback, Robin Earl. Earl picked up yardage and scored, but the extra point was blocked. With less than thirty seconds to play the Giants tied the score 9–9 with a field goal. The game went into sudden death overtime.

The teams traded the ball several times and Chicago missed two field goals. There was only 1:30 left in the overtime period. A tie would keep the Bears out of the playoffs. "We were freezing, soaked and tired," Payton said, "but we still had a chance if we could just get the ball." The Bears' defense held and the Giants punted. The return man fumbled the kick but recovered just past midfield. Avellini hit Greg Latta with two quick passes to the Giant 25-yard line. There were 42 seconds left on the clock.

On the next play after a Bear timeout, Avellini threw to Payton, hoping he'd step out of bounds to stop the clock. But when he caught the ball, only Giants' defensive back Larry Mallory was between him and a better field goal position. In that instant Payton showed his greatness. He cut toward the open field and eluded Mallory. Slipping and sliding, he was tackled on the 11-yard line. The Bear field goal unit rushed on the field in what looked like a Mack Sennett Keystone Kop chase, and Bob Thomas booted it through—for a playoff spot.

Payton gained only 47 yards rushing and told the writers, "I'll take those fourteen yards on that pass play over any rushing record." Then he paused and his frozen face slowly eased into a mischievous grin. "I don't say I could have done it on a dry field—but it sure would have been fun to try."

He had fallen short, gaining 1,852 yards on a record 339 carries, and had a superb 5.5 average. It was the third highest total in NFL history behind Simpson and Brown. If it hadn't been for the weather, he certainly would have passed Brown and possibly Simpson. More important to him, "The Bears proved they could win without my having an exceptional day. We proved we could run up a record as good as the Vikings. We proved we were a never-say-die winning team."

The week before playing powerful Dallas in the first play-off game, Payton was in bed with the flu. A friend called to ask his condition, and Payton said it was good that athletes sometimes get a chance to understand how really fortunate they were, "because when we feel bad, we realize how easy it is to forget really unfortunate people sick at home or in the hospital during the Christmas holiday." He mentioned a Wheaton, Illinois, high school player who had broken his neck and to whom he had dedicated the Giants game. He said it was important that "we give 100 percent of ourselves to help the less fortunate."

Despite his flu, Payton was eager for the playoff game against the Dallas Cowboys. The Bears thought they might have a psychological edge as underdog to a powerhouse team that rarely lost in their home stadium. But their optimism blinded them to the toll taken by just getting into the play-offs. They had used every reserve of energy and were a physically battered and exhausted team. They didn't go into the game intimidated by the Cowboys and didn't play hesitantly.

But they were whipped 37–7. Dallas, the essence of great football when they were on their game, was awesome that day. Cowboy coach Tom Landry, rarely given to super-latives, said it was one of their best performances ever. Early in the game the Cowboys made their only mistakes and fumbled twice, but the Bears couldn't do anything against the strong Dallas defense. Their only score came late in the fourth quarter. Payton gained only 61 yards on 19 carries. "We just had it taken to us." Dallas safety Cliff Harris, one of football's most punishing hitters, came away with a vivid memory of Payton's ability to take a blow. "I nailed him as he was turning to catch a pass, one of the hardest hits I've ever delivered, and he just bounced up and tapped me on the helmet." But Payton suffered a concussion in the fourth quarter and barely remembered the rest of the game. He later said there was little consolation that they had been beaten by the best. Dallas went on to beat Denver in Super Bowl XII for the NFL championship.

In only three seasons Payton owned 2 NFL rushing records, shared 14 Bears' records, and needed just one more 100-yard game to tie Sayers with 20. In 1977 he led the NFL with 16 touchdowns. He led in carries (339), yards (1,852, then the third highest ever), and average per carry (5.5) to win the NFL rushing title. He had played in 37 consecutive games and needed only 1,737 yards to break the Bears' career mark of 5,657 set by Rick Casares in ten years. He owned 6 of the top 11 rushing days in Bears' history.

Payton was named the United Press International Athlete of the Year and was the only *unanimous* choice for the Pro Bowl. The Pro Football Writers of America named him NFL Most Valuable Player. He won the Thorpe Trophy and was the Associated Press Player of the Year and Offensive Player of the Year. *Sporting News* and *Sport Magazine* gave him their NFL Player of the Year award. He was the leading vote-getter to the United Press All-National Conference team.

He would go on to be named to the Pro Bowl nine times, a record shared by only three other all-time greats: defensive tackle Joe Greene and linebacker Jack Lambert of the Pittsburgh Steelers, and Ken Houston, a strong safety who played with Houston and Washington. Playing against the league's best in the Pro Bowl, Payton holds records for most carries (81) and most yards gained (368). He is second in highest average gain per game for at least ten attempts: 6.9 to O. J. Simpson's and Ottis Anderson's 7.

WALTER PAYTON WAS NOW ESTABLISHED as one of the NFL's greatest players and continued his long assault on almost every rushing record in the book.

In 1978 Neill Armstrong was named head coach to replace Jack Pardee, who had left. The Bears won their first three games, then lost eight in a row and finished at 7–9 in the first 16-game schedule. Payton became the first Chicago runner to rush for more than 1,000 yards in three consecutive years. He led the National Conference with 1,395 yards and was second in the league to Earl Campbell of the Houston Oilers. Payton was happy for Roland Harper, his best friend and backfield mate, who had his best season with 992 yards. And the season ended with promise. The Bears won four of their last five games and had a good draft—defensive tackle Dan Hampton, defensive end Al Harris, and wide receiver Ricky Watts.

In the off-season, Payton competed in television's "Superstars" program and injured himself on the obstacle course. He hit a blocking sled so hard it lifted off the ground and rocked back on its steel runners and sliced his knee to the bone. But he still set a course record. Despite a rash of serious injuries, the Bears had an excellent 10–6 season in 1979. "We learned to be winners," Payton said. They were beaten by the Philadelphia Eagles in the first round of the playoffs, a game many felt the Bears should have won but for some controversial calls by the officials. Payton had his fourth consecutive 1,000-yard season (1,610), led the National Conference for the fourth consecutive year and again was second in the league to Earl Campbell. The draft brought linebacker Otis Wilson and fullback Matt Suhey, and for the first time in fifteen years the Bears were picked to win their division.

In the 1980 season opener, they stumbled against Green Bay on a scorching day. Both teams plodded into overtime with a 6–6 tie. Chester Marcol, the Packers' place-kicker, tried a 34-yard field goal. The kick was blocked—and bounced right back to Marcol, who ran it in for the winning touchdown. The freak loss seemed to set the tone for the entire season. In the second game against Tampa Bay, Payton was in top form. He gained 183 yards, the fourth best of his career, and scored on a 69-yard run, his longest ever. His 10.2 average per carry was also a career high. They took a 34–14 beating in the Vikings game and were destroyed 38–3 by the Steelers, the reigning Super Bowl champs.

In the fifth game against Tampa Bay, Payton set another Bears' record. Just into his sixth season, his career combined yards—running and pass receptions—surpassed Sayers's 9,435. There were a few other season highlights for Payton. Against Washington he caught a 54-yard touchdown pass and scored on a 50-yard run. In the fourteenth game, the Bears avenged the humiliating loss to Green Bay. They whipped the Packers 61–7, the most points scored by one team in an NFL game since 1973. Payton had a fifth consecutive 1,000-yard season (1,460) and his fifth Conference crown, and once more was second to Campbell. He was the only Bears' player selected to the Pro Bowl. The honor was empty to Payton. The team had slipped to 7–9, and he wondered if he was one of those athletes doomed to star for a constant loser. The Bears had another prosperous draft: offensive tackle Keith Van Horne, linebacker Mike Singletary, and safety Tod Bell. The nucleus of the great Bear teams of the mid-1980s was gathering.

The 1981 season brought even less success on the field, a 6–10 record. Payton had, what was for him, only an ordinary season: 1,000 yards (1,222) for the sixth straight year, his 3.6 average per carry well below his career mark of 4.5. He ranked seventh in the Conference in a golden age of wonderful runners: George Rogers (Saints), Tony Dorsett (Cowboys), Billy Sims (Lions), Wilbert Montgomery (Eagles), Ottis Anderson (Cardinals), and William Andrews (Falcons). Payton made no excuses, but one day after three straight sub-100 yard games, he stalked out of the locker room, muttering:

"I took a beating. The first week I could understand it; we had a rookie at tackle. But last week I took a beating and this week I took a beating. There's only so much you can take. If the rest of the season's going to be like this, the linemen can start scavenging for my arms and legs. . . ."

When asked to elaborate, Payton referred all questions to coach Armstrong, who quickly blamed the linemen:

"Walter is gang-tackled every game. He better be gang-tackled or the other team will have a hard time, because Walter is as good a running back as there is in football. But

104

he has to have the people up front blocking for him . . . there is nothing wrong with Walter Payton at all."

Later that week, Payton said, "It got to the point where there wasn't any place to go. I had to attack the defense because there was no place to run. I broke my shoulder pads. Look at my helmet. Sure, I'd like to keep my consecutive game streak going. But more important, I'd like to be standing up at my retirement press conference, whenever that is."

The next week, Payton said he was proud of his linemen. They hadn't given him a lot more room, but at least, he said, they were playing hard on every down. He went five games without a 100-yard day, the longest drought since his rookie year of 1975. Despite the poor season and the outburst he regretted, that year brought him his greatest private joy: his first child, a son named Jarrett.

George Halas took measures to bring the Bears back to their glory days. Despite Payton, the offense, particularly under Neill Armstrong, had no punch or imagination. In Payton's seven years, the Bears' passing attack never ranked better than 24th in a 28-team league. After the 1981 season Halas brought in Mike Ditka as head coach. Ditka, then an assistant coach with Dallas, was a former Bear and Cowboy tight end, a four-time all-pro. He was tough, without fear, and ready to be a head coach. He vowed to bring to Chicago some of the Cowboys' fabled offense. The Bears needed an offensive general and a locker room butt-kicker, and Ditka was perfect for the role. And he was an emotional and visible link to the last Bears' championship team. In addition to Ditka, another fierce competitor was added in the 1982 draft. Quarterback Jim McMahon, a colorful player with a cool, reckless temperament, joined a growing cast of rowdies and eccentrics, all superb athletes.

105

When he was a Bear player, Ditka's style was to pin team-mates on the locker room wall if they didn't meet his standards. Religion later tamed his temper, but at first he was little different as a coach. "When the players walked in the first day," recalled Payton, "Mike was standing there with his arms folded. He nodded to an assistant who called the roll. I thought, 'We're in the army now.'" Ditka broke tables, and once in a fury after a loss broke his hand punching a blackboard. He grabbed players on the sideline and yelled at them, threw clipboards, cursed officials. But slowly he began to instill excellence and pride in his players. "Some teams are named Smith," Ditka said, "some are named Grabowski." He ran his finger over his moustache and had a snarling smile. "We're the Grabowskis." He quickly became a Payton admirer:

"I thought Walter was one hell of a football player before I came to the Bears. I had great admiration for him. He was tough, always gave something extra when he was about to be tackled. When I got here I saw what an athlete he was . . . his strength, you can't believe it. Nobody realizes how big he is under there. He plays like he weighs 240. He's the very best football player I've ever seen. Period. At any position. Period. He's a complete player. He will run, throw, receive, block for you. There are a lot of great running backs, but Walter is a great citizen as well . . . I think he gives back to the game as much as he takes out. Those qualities alone would make him something special."

Under McMahon, the Bears began to pass more in a complex, sophisticated offense. The attack was no longer focused only on Payton, but Ditka explained that his halfback was still the key element. "I try to get the ball into Walter's hands as many times as I can either running, catching, or throwing. I don't want to build an offense around one man, except I'm not stupid enough not to use the best tool I have as effectively as I can. I like to run the football. I think you have to."

Instead of his career average 21 carries a game, Payton, in his first season under Ditka, averaged just 16 carries a game, his lowest since his rookie year. The sports media, quick to stir a player-coach dispute, asked Payton if he was unhappy in his lesser role, did it affect his attitude. He juked as effectively as he did on the field and didn't like saying anything that might cause discord on the team. But he could turn surly and question Ditka's way of using him. After a game when he had only 13 carries, he said dryly, "Terrific game plan." McMahon, though new to the team, understood Payton. "If it starts to work, I think he'll enjoy it. He's just been frustrated for so long. If we win it'll be different. When you're successful, there's not too many unhappy people."

No one expected the turnaround to be instantaneous. McMahon was only a rookie quarterback, and his development was stopped by a seven-week players' strike. During the strike, unlike the one in 1987, there were no replacement teams and it was only a nine-game schedule. McMahon didn't start until the first game after the strike and quickly showed the cocky leadership that would take Chicago out of the desert. He completed 16 of 27 passes for 233 yards and 2 touchdowns against Detroit, and one long pass set up the winning field goal. With McMahon at quarterback, the team went 3–4 the rest of the way.

In nine games Payton rushed for a somewhat disappointing 596 yards on 148 attempts. Ditka's first year as head coach produced a 3–6 record in a season filled with turmoil and a long interruption in the schedule. It was hardly a fair test for any new coach. The 1983 draft was especially productive: offensive linemen Jim Covert and Mark Bortz, defensive end Richard Dent, wide receivers Willie Gault and Dennis McKinnon, defensive backs Dave Duerson and Mike Richardson. The addition of those seven players would make the Bears a wild, inspired, dominant team that harked back to their great days. And at last Payton had a cast of players formidable enough to support his art.

In 1983 the team went 8–8 and Payton had one of his best seasons. In the second game against Tampa Bay he caught a 62-yard touchdown pass. In the third against the Saints he threw two touchdown passes to Willie Gault and ran 49 yards for another. In the tenth game against the Rams he took a lateral from McMahon on a razzle-dazzle play, then threw to the quarterback for a touchdown. He rushed for 1,421 yards and caught 53 passes, more than any other Bears' player. Adding to his happiness was a new daughter, Brittney.

In 1984 the Bears began their climb. They went 10–6, won the division title for the first time since 1963, and made the playoffs. A season highlight came in the sixth game against the New Orleans Saints, when Payton broke Jim Brown's "unbreakable" rushing record. Tom Weir, a sports columnist for *USA Today* wrote:

"Sadly, Payton might join the Cubs as a Chicago symbol of sports futility. He is a 1980s version of Mister Cub, Ernie Banks—a great player who never wore a World Series ring. There is a little of Roger Maris in Payton, too. Just as Maris had to wear an asterisk beside his name for hitting his homers in 162 games, instead of 154 like Babe Ruth, statisticians are already sullying Payton's record because Brown amassed his 12,312 yards in 18 fewer games."

Payton, however, wasn't bothered and was still the practical joker and cutup who kept things light. Dan Rains, a reserve linebacker, thought a bee had flown into the earhole

Walter Payton with his daughter, Brittney. *Courtesy of Chicago Sun-Times, Inc./Photo by Sun-Times Photographer.*

of his helmet during a break in practice. He ripped it off and found a piece of paper and spotted Payton alternately buzzing and giggling. Rains' reaction: "I appreciate that I'll be able to tell my grandchildren that I played with the best there ever was."

"I don't think people realize what a great sense of humor Walter has," said Matt Suhey, "an ability to say or do something funny at the right time. I dropped a pass against the Colts and on the way back to the huddle he said to me, 'You can always get a paper route or join the army.' And he's a good mimic. He does a great Ditka and a great Buckwheat from the Little Rascals."

The Bears went into the playoffs severely handicapped. Jim McMahon was out with an injury suffered when he scrambled against the Raiders. To make matters worse, they faced the potent 11–5 Washington Redskins, winners of the Eastern Division. Washington scored first with a field goal, but the Bears tied it in the second quarter. They went ahead when Payton lofted a 19-yard pass to the tight end. Willie Gault caught a 75-yard touchdown pass; then Dennis McKinnon scored on another pass to put the game away. The Bears next played the San Francisco Forty-Niners for the National Conference championship, only a step away from the Super Bowl.

The Forty-Niners were an offensive powerhouse, with Joe Montana throwing to a corps of superior receivers and two fine runners in Roger Craig and Wendell Tyler. The Bears' defense kept them in the game in the first half, allowing only two San Francisco field goals. But the Forty-Niners also had the best defense in the league that year and the Bears went scoreless in a 23–0 defeat. Walking off the field after the game, Ronnie Lott, a Forty-Niner safety, told the Bears to "bring your offense next time." It was a loss the Bears wouldn't soon forget and gleefully avenged the next year.

With another fine draft—defensive tackle William "The Refrigerator" Perry, linebacker Wilber Marshall, running backs Neal Anderson and Thomas Sanders, defensive back Reggie Phillips, placekicker Kevin Butler—all the building blocks were in place. Chicago won its first five games and in the sixth redeemed themselves against the Forty-Niners with a 26–10 victory. They did more than beat the Forty-Niners; they beat them up, sacked Montana five times, and held them to 183 total yards, the lowest ever for coach Bill Walsh's high-gear offense. It was sweet revenge. After the game Ronnie Lott said, "Walter Payton's got a heart as big as any player I've ever come across." Payton rushed for 132 yards in that game, and 192 the next week against Green Bay, his best since he gained the same number against Kansas City in 1977.

In the eleventh game of 1985 the Bears walloped Dallas 44–0, and Payton posted his ninth 1,000-yard season. The Bears went undefeated in their first twelve games, but their dream of perfection died in the thirteenth against the Miami Dolphins in a 38–24 loss. In that game Payton set still another record, rushing for more than 100 yards in eight consecutive games. He made it nine the following week against the Colts. He was football's leading career rusher, but he also led in other less-noticed aspects of the game—throwing crushing blocks to protect a quarterback or spring another runner, and making full-fledged fakes into the line to freeze one set of defenders and free up other parts of the field.

With a 15–1 record they had home field advantage for the playoffs in the frigid Chicago winter called "Bear weather." On a freezing, blustery day the Bears whipped the New York Giants 21–0. They were an 11-point favorite over the Los Angeles Rams, despite the presence of Eric Dickerson, the best young runner in the league. The Rams also had a stout defense, but the Bears played one of their most dominating games. They held Dickerson to 46 yards and the Rams to a paltry 130 total yards in a 24–0 win. To a man the Bears desperately wanted to take on Miami in Super Bowl XX in the New Orleans Superdome, but Miami was defeated by the New England Patriots, who became the Bears' opponent for the NFL championship. On the eve of the game, Payton said, "If it took me ten years to get here, there will be no return. Tomorrow isn't promised to anybody. You have to take full advantage of what you have to deal with." The Bears destroyed the Patriots 46–10, the most lopsided victory in Super Bowl history.

Despite winning the championship, there was a sour note in the game. It was assumed that when the Bears had a shot at a rushing touchdown, Payton would be given the ball. He had been the heart of the team for so long, had played in losing causes for so many years, it was felt he deserved the honor. He was thirty-one-years-old, and who knew how much longer he could play or when Chicago might again reach the Super Bowl. But when the opportunity came for an almost certain short-yardage touchdown, McMahon handed off to Matt Suhey, perfectly good strategy by Ditka because the Patriots would be keying on Payton.

Payton was silent and grim-faced after the game. He disappeared from the Bears' locker room, then returned half an hour later to a makeshift interview area. After much prodding by reporters, he admitted that he was sad and disappointed, then walked off with his son. Many people speculated that he was upset about not scoring a touchdown.

"It wasn't the touchdown," Payton later said. "It was a lot of things coming together that I don't want to get into right now. Basically the Super Bowl was anticlimactic for me. The game was dull."

Bear center Jay Hilgenberg tried to put any "controversy"

to rest. He said he didn't hear any special talk—in the huddle or on the sideline—about getting the ball to Payton for a close-in touchdown. "He didn't score? I didn't even know. He's the greatest. He doesn't need a Super Bowl touchdown to be the greatest."

It could have been the toll of a full eleven seasons, along with the postseason chaos, but it began to appear that Payton had all the boy beaten out of him. Aside from the forged body he maintained like a vintage Dusenberg, pride, good sense, and luck played major roles in his longevity. Although he avoided the career-ending injury, he wasn't immune to the ravages of the game. He had arthroscopic surgery on both knees in 1984. He played much of 1985 in pain with a sore shoulder and torn rib cartilage. He played with cracked ribs, high fever, and a dislocated toe, the latter an injury that would bench almost any other runner, but he didn't miss a minute of playing time. Each year the pains lingered longer and accumulated. Payton responded by stepping up his off-season conditioning to maintain his expected level. That Super Bowl year, Leslie Frazier, a Bear cornerback, said, "If you didn't know who he was, you'd look at him and ask, 'Who's that twenty-two-year-old rookie?'"

It's a question of which deserted him first, his body or his desire. Over the years he made a habit of hinting that the next season or two might be his last. Back in 1977 he adamantly stated that he wouldn't play past five seasons, that he didn't want the game to debilitate him. He wanted to pursue other things, maybe a dancing career. Reminded of the prediction, Payton smiled. "I was kind of wild. I just said those things to keep people off me. If I said, 'I'm going to play eleven or twelve or thirteen seasons,' people would think I'm crazy. I'm just protecting myself. I don't let anyone know what's going on in my head."

Friends and fellow-players speculated about how long he would play, and his 1985 performance made most of them optimistic. He gained 1,551 yards with a 4.8 average, second only to his 5.5 in 1977, his most productive year.

"He has desire and love of the game," said tackle Jim Covert. "I sure don't see any sign of him slowing down. He can play as long as he wants."

Johnny Roland, Bears' backfield coach, was dead serious when he said he thought that Payton could play until he was forty.

"Body-wise, I would say yes he can. It would depend on what speed he lost. He hasn't lost any quickness. The whole thing is Walter's enthusiasm. Once that enthusiasm wanes, he'll just pack up his gear, go away happily and say, 'I had a great career.'"

Bill Tobin, the Bears' personnel director, said, "Walter was never quite as fast as he thought he was"—meaning that a slight loss of speed wouldn't be the determining factor. "But he's a complete phenomenon and the best player I've ever seen or hope to see."

But there was a real factor that would influence Payton's retirement. In 1986 the Bears selected Florida running back Neal Anderson as their number one back. A blazer with power who could also catch passes and block, he was the first threat to Payton's supremacy. Thomas Sanders was another fine young runner who waited in the wings. Matt Suhey stated flatly, "There's nobody on the field with a bigger ego than Walter. I can't see him sharing time with anybody."

Payton put Anderson's career as a regular on hold in 1986 by running for 1,333 yards to finish fifth in the NFL, and only one back, Seattle's Curt Warner, caught more passes. But he constantly heard talk that he should hang it up and make room for Anderson and Sanders. He fumbled more often toward the end of the 1986 season, including a critical drop in the playoff loss to Washington. Experts said he'd lost a step or two, could no longer sweep wide. They said Anderson hit the hole and turned the corner faster than Payton.

"People won't say it to my face, but you hear mumblings," Payton said. "I remember times when it wasn't me they were on. It was other players and it was unjust . . . I'm not a good judge of myself. Everybody wants to think they're as good as when they first came in. You might be slowing down in areas and might not see it, but other people do. When even fans suggest that you retire, it hurts, but what can you do."

The whispers and criticism, the premature burial did seem unjust. Yet going into the 1987 season Payton would be thirty-three, Anderson twenty-three. Youth had to be served someday, and probably sooner than Payton would have liked. There were suggestions that he play more fullback, and he said it didn't make much difference. But others suspected he was reluctant to take the job away from friends Matt Suhey and Calvin Thomas.

"I know you can't maintain what you have forever," Payton said graciously. "I work hard. I'm happy to be where I am, even to be competing with young guys like that and holding my own. It's a thrill to hear people argue, 'I think Neal should be playing,' or 'I think Walter should be playing.' I've been here for twelve years. I'm an old man."

Payton didn't feel old, but he understood the facts of football life and longevity, seemed to have come to terms with the inevitable: "How would I feel about a reduced role? If they feel I'm not contributing enough, then please tell me. I'll be gone. I'll try my wares somewhere else. Because when I feel I don't want to play anymore or that I'm not as effective, I'll be the first to tell them."

115

At the Pro Bowl in Hawaii his competitive form flamed again. For the first time his remarks sometimes sounded sour and self-serving, the plaint of an athlete superior and dominant for so long that he couldn't imagine anything could change: "Neal Anderson looks real good. He's physical, big enough. He'll be playing a lot and he should. But if Neal or Sanders want my job, or if somebody they draft wants my job, they'll have to lead the league in everything and be the most valuable player because I'm going to work my butt off to attain that. If Eric Dickerson played for the Bears, I'd push him damn hard. And if he was better than me, he'd be the greatest football player who ever was because I'd be pushing him that hard.

"For so long people took me for granted. Now they have a guy who comes in for a few plays in special situations. Who's doing the blocking for him? It's different when you play from the start and everybody is fresh and everybody is kicking butts. It's harder. I'm like the Marines. Put me in there to do the hard work. Look at all the hits I take. If the fans ruin my fun, I'll leave. If it goes bad—if one moment of the coming year isn't as good as I thought it would be—I won't tarnish the twelve years I've had. I want to go out on a high note. I don't want to be remembered just as a statistic."

Then, almost sadly: "What hurts is how people slight me now."

Money was no consideration. In 1986 the last year of a three-year contract paid him $685,000. He had an annuity from the Bears that would pay him $240,000 a year for the rest of his life. He had many business interests, owned three nightclubs that alone brought him $400,000 a year. He planned eight more around the country, including Hawaii and Japan. At the Pro Bowl he carried a phone around the lobby to tend to business affairs. Commercials and personal appearances paid well. He often refused those he didn't think suitable: "I turned down one for chewing tobacco. It wasn't me. Those people spit in a cup. That's not my image." He once turned down an extremely generous movie offer because it interfered with a spring minicamp, though the Bears would have been happy to excuse him.

Payton was such a model citizen it was hard to imagine Chicago, let alone the Bears, without him. He did volunteer work for many civic organizations and charities. On his own he threw benefits for sick and needy children, played with the healthy and consoled the troubled. Early in his career he told the Bears' public relations office always to let him know if there was anything he could do for children. And at a time when a number of pro athletes were engaged in court battles or sex and drug scandals, Payton was a model for young people. His chief vice seemed to be lighting firecrackers, his favorite drug probably a cheeseburger. When asked which political party he belongs to, he says, "I'm an American."

When the Bears opened their 1987 training camp, Mike Ditka was asked who his best running back was. He hesitated, then said:

"Walter Payton is my best football player."

It was a neat, diplomatic way of avoiding controversy and not ruffling Payton's feelings. To the writers covering the team, Ditka had made it clear: Neal Anderson, used sparingly the year before, was now the best runner on the team. It was a question of youth. Chicago had gone 14–2 in the 1986 regular season but played poorly in the NFC championship game against Washington. They didn't reach the Super Bowl and Ditka was determined not to let that happen again. Also implicit in his statement was the fact that Payton was still an important cog in the team but would play a lesser role.

Observers noticed something different in Payton's manner that summer. He seemed more reflective, talked about how "hard it will be to say good-bye. I've been doing this all my life. I'll miss the game, but what I'll miss most is the camaraderie." He talked about how he'd like to go out.

"I'd like to throw a party in a stadium, have a free concert, invite fans and friends and entertainers . . . sit down in front of people . . . then at the end shake hands with each and every one that wants to."

He was still the team cheerleader and mischievous joker. One day the writers came into the locker room and saw Payton on a table, his ankle encased in an inflatable, rubberized cast and resting on a styrofoam mold.

"Come on, Walter," said a writer familiar with Payton's pranks. "In about two seconds you'll get up and jump over a building or something."

"You guys didn't believe me when I said I was quitting," said Payton, his face somber. "You didn't believe me when I said I was gay. Now you don't believe me when I say my ankle's broken."

It wasn't, of course. He started his 169th straight game against the New York Giants in the 1987 season opener. He suffered a bad ankle sprain in the first quarter, had it rewrapped, returned to the game and carried 18 times for 42 yards, caught 2 passes for 12. One writer called it "a ho-hum day for Walter." Typically, Payton didn't blame the ankle injury. Neal Anderson's 62 yards on 13 carries, 6 catches for 81, many of them key plays in the victory over the Giants, was an eye opener for the writers.

Was the future already here? Had Payton lost a step not only on the field but also on his pedestal? Was one of the fabled runners in NFL history fated to end his career as the number 2 runner on his own team?

The writers kept prodding Payton—after only one game!—about giving up his role to Anderson.

"Why do you ask questions like that?" Payton's eyes flashed. "Are you just trying to aggravate me?"

When the locker room interview ended, Payton, his voice soft, said, "You guys want to do me a favor?" They expected a plea to stop writing about his reduced role and how he reacted to it . . . Anderson's performance and the way he turned a short pass into a 47-yard gain . . . how it might have made him feel old.

But Payton, barely suppressing a laugh as he pretended to grimace in pain from the ankle injury, said, "Please carry me to my car."

Football realists saw that it was inevitable: Payton would begin to surrender to time and to Neal Anderson. Backfield coach Johnny Roland put it kindly if bluntly: "Neal led the team in rushing in preseason and that's a pretty good indication. Walter will still, hopefully, get his 1,000 yards. I'd like to think we'll have two 1,000-yard rushers by season's end."

The conventional wisdom was that Payton would benefit by having his work load cut. "Last year," said Roland, "we wore his butt out because we called on him so much. We're trying to keep Walter fresh as we go down through the year. He doesn't have to carry the burden on his shoulders anymore. Usually, if a defense stopped Walter, they stopped the Bears. Not anymore."

The coaches expected no whining or trouble from Payton. He had always prided himself on being the ultimate team player. Through the years he'd always been a sort of mother hen with other running backs. "He pulls them into his nest, he teaches and watches over them," said Roland.

Payton was a question mark for the second game, but he was making a different kind of news. His dream was to be the first black owner of a National Football League franchise. Payton hoped to do it in 1990, when the NFL expects to add

120

Payton, who practically reinvented the stiff arm, warding off a Washington Redskins tackler. *Courtesy of Chicago Sun-Times, Inc./Photo by Sun-Times Photographer.*

two more expansion teams. He and his business advisers had already met with NFL Commissioner Pete Rozelle about that possibility. He announced that if he owned a team he'd like to hire either Mike Ditka or Johnny Roland as head coach. If he got the team and hired Roland, he would be the first black owner with the first black coach. "It would not be a racial thing," he said. "Color has nothing to do with it." The price of an established NFL franchise could be as much as $100 million, and a new franchise could go well above that. Payton estimated his own worth at $16 million, but two investors had each offered $70 million.

"The deal can be done, I'm confident of that," said Payton, who will insist on holding a majority interest. "It's just a question of working out the details. I was approached by people in London who wanted to start a pro football league there. I thought about it, then asked myself why should I go abroad to fulfill a dream I had here all my life. I've accomplished everything I can at the player level. I want to take that next step and make my mark there. I've never been a guy to 'settle' for things. I'm not going to change now. I'm a goal-oriented person and this is my goal."

It is still only a goal and a dream. Nothing has been signed. Rozelle made no promises. No sites have been picked for the two new teams. But Payton's reputation around the league is in his favor. He has the capital to do it and the enthusiastic backing of many owners. Art Modell, owner of the Cleveland Browns, sees Payton's bid as a giant step forward for the NFL. The league's players are about 60 percent black, but there are no black owners or head coaches. Modell said; "I can't think of anything more dramatic for blacks in sports than to assume a minority or majority ownership. So the fact that Walter Payton has expressed interest in owning a team someplace, sometime, is exciting."

Payton had not flatly declared that the 1987 season would be his last, but he kept dropping several broad hints despite a hedging "nothing is final." But what was there left for him to achieve? At season's start he held seven NFL records and soon set two more. He had his Super Bowl ring. His place in football history was secure. Some critics, however, thought it presumptuous of Payton to want a franchise. What did he know about running a team?

"I have my own ideas about how a franchise should be run. I'm anxious to try them out, see how they work." Payton said there would be no front-office feuds and dissension as he had seen with the Bears and other teams. "I'll stress teamwork in the front office. It's no place for dueling egos. I've been around the game a long time. I think I've learned a few things. I understand what a player wants from management—commitment, consistency, communication. I could bring that to the owner's role.

"I'd work with players. But I won't be a soft touch. I'll be a tough negotiator. I have a pretty good idea of what a player is worth and what's fair. I worked for my money. I'll expect those players to work, too. I've been a competitor all my life. I'll be a competitor and an executive, too. The only difference is I won't be sore on Mondays." He made an offhand comment about getting old as a player. "Let's put it this way. When I first started playing football, I didn't use near as much adhesive tape as I do now."

He didn't allow the ownership business to distract him on the field. In the second game against Tampa Bay, running on a sore ankle, he broke another NFL record—the 106 rushing touchdowns he shared with Jim Brown. But he gained only 24 yards on 15 carries, caught two passes, one for a second touchdown. Neal Anderson ran for 115 yards and a touchdown on 16 carries, and had 4 catches for 28 yards.

The National Football League Players' Association went on strike after the second game. There were no games the third week. Then the League played three games—that would count in the standings—with replacement teams. It bred great ill-feeling as the owners took a hard line, and there was dissension on many teams when regular players began to break the picket line to go in and play. The Players' Association finally caved in to management and went back to work. Payton kept a low profile during the strike. The Bears' team was solid in its support for the strike, and no player returned until the walkout was over. There was no discord on the team when regular play resumed for what would be a 15-game schedule.

The Bears' first post-strike game was again with Tampa Bay, a division opponent. The Bucs, a young team, surprisingly jumped off to a 20–0 lead. But Jim McMahon, playing his first game since being injured the year before, drove the Bears to a slim 27–26 victory. Payton carried only six times—because Chicago had to pass more to come from behind—and gained 30 yards for a good 5-yard average. He caught two passes for no gain. Anderson carried only six times and gained 52 yards, 38 on a touchdown run, and caught 7 passes for 45 yards and a second touchdown, the game-winner with only 1:30 left on the clock.

In the Kansas City game, Payton gained only 15 yards on 8 carries. Anderson had a mediocre day, and in the next two games against Green Bay and Denver, Payton outgained him. But it was clear that Anderson had become the Bears' chief offensive threat. No one had any illusions that Payton would suddenly bloom again, turn the clock back, and be the runner he once was. He would play good, dependable football and still be a great part of the team's spirit—all that was expected of him.

During the Green Bay game, television announcers John Madden and Pat Summerall talked about the Payton situation, about whether younger players should be given more of a chance. They agreed that Ditka would not make a change because Payton had lost a step or two. He had flatly said, "I'm just not going to do it. I'm elated with the job he's doing." But Madden and Summerall, however much they admired Payton—and Madden had called him the best back in football history—implied that it was time for a change. In that game Payton caught a pass that set up a touchdown. He was taken out for Thomas Sanders near the goal line. Sanders was racked up for no gain on a sweep. On 4th and 1 for a touchdown, Payton was back in the game and scored on one of his patented leaps over the line.

The Denver game was on Monday Night Football. Before the game it was announced that there would be a telephone poll to determine "the best runner ever." The voting would continue throughout the game and the results given at the end. The featured runners were Walter Payton, Gale Sayers, Jim Brown, O. J. Simpson, and a catchall "others." Surprisingly, Payton led the voting with a whopping 46 percent. Brown had 29 percent, Simpson 11, Sayers only 7, the same as "others." No one took the poll seriously. Payton was still active—playing that very night—and had constant media attention, while the others had been retired for years. It was a measure of the public's short memory and/or ignorance that the three other legends combined could only garner 47 percent of the vote, merely a point better than Payton. But it was also a tribute to a unique athlete who had thrilled them, given his all on every play in every game for thirteen seasons.

Payton gained 73 yards against Denver. He seemed quicker than he had all season, running with something of his old fierceness. He broke another NFL record—for receptions by a running back—with his 476th catch, erasing New York Giant Tony Galbreath's mark. After the Detroit game, the seventh played by the regulars, he edged into fifteenth place among NFC rushers—293 yards on 84 carries for a 3.5 average. Anderson ranked seventh—423 yards on 89 carries for a 4.8 average. Against the Packers and Vikings Payton had decent games, but no more than any good back could have produced. He was still blocking like a man possessed but missing quick defenders more often.

Gale Sayers appeared on a New York radio sports program and insisted that Payton should retire because "he has lost two steps." Then he said what everyone felt but no one had dared to say: "Walter knows when it comes to crunch time, they're going to go to Anderson or Gentry or Sanders."

"*Walter Payton is fading away from us,*" was the lead sentence in a Chicago sports column. Payton said it was his last season and wouldn't change his mind. What he didn't say was that his running suffered because he didn't have a blocker like himself leading the way. With Anderson starting, fullback Matt Suhey, Payton's sturdy blocker for years, had only limited playing time. In mid-November Payton could no longer contain himself. He told reporters that he was frustrated by his changing role with the Bears and thought about playing for another team. "PAYTON'S TORMENT" was the Chicago *Sun-Times* headline.

"Sometimes I feel I'm the problem here," he said. "A lot of times I feel I don't even belong here. These are feelings I never had before. It's hard."

He talked of retiring before season's end. To Payton, who wanted to go out on a high note, the situation had to be demeaning—to want to do better, to know truthfully that he could do better, but only rarely showing flashes of his old self. Chicago's other fine running backs were his friends and he felt he was in their way. On another team he wouldn't have worried about it. His poor start had complicated matters and he might be happier with another team, renew his interest in the game. "Right now," he said, "I don't feel appreciated."

Mike Tomczak, backup Bears' quarterback, said all Payton needed was a good game in which the team depended on him. "He's still the player who makes the Bears click. The story isn't ended yet. There are still many pages to turn." Johnny Roland was surprised Payton hadn't gone public before. "He's a very sensitive guy." Jim McMahon tried to explain Payton's limited role. "Walter doesn't feel part of the offense anymore. But we've fallen behind too many times this year and haven't had the ball often. When we did, we had to pass to catch up."

Payton had risked creating dissension on the team. It was uncharacteristic of a man who thought of himself as the ultimate team player. Worse, it seemed a sad case of ego for Payton who had played at the peak for so long and now was in his last season. But after the brief flurry there were no more statements by him or anyone else.

In the second game against the Vikings, a division opponent, they were behind again as the clock ran down. It took a thrilling last-minute pass play for a touchdown to pull out a 30–24 victory. Confidence was high before the Monday night game with San Francisco. The experts said it would be a preview of the NFC championship game, deciding who would go to the Super Bowl. Both teams came in at 10–2, and the winner would almost surely have the home field advantage for the playoffs.

In the pressbox before the game, one writer turned to the others: "I know it's unprofessional as hell, but just once more I want to see Payton have a great game—see one of those runs where he's knocked around like a pinball and breaking tackles for big yardage. And I have a hunch he's going to do it tonight. It's a big game—his kind of game."

But he was thinking of another Walter Payton, in another game, in another time. The "crucial" game was a disaster for the Bears. Jim McMahon was out with a leg injury. Then Joe Montana, the Forty-Niners' quarterback, went down with a

Payton putting a vicious block on a Green Bay defender. *Courtesy of Chicago Sun-Times, Inc./Photo by Sun-Times Photographer.*

pulled hamstring midway through the first quarter. Chicago seemed to have the advantage, with a more experienced backup in Mike Tomczak. Steve Young, the Forty-Niners' backup, had only thrown seven passes all season.

The Bears played poorly from the start. Tomczak threw four interceptions in the first half and was replaced by rookie Jim Harbaugh. Young had his finest game as a pro with four touchdown passes. The Bears also lost two fumbles, one by Payton deep in their own territory. He took a pitchout and carried the ball high and loose with one hand as he swept left. A Forty-Niner linebacker punched it out of Payton's hand before he could tuck it away. It led to a Forty-Niners' touchdown.

Payton gained only 18 yards on 7 carries in a humiliating 41–0 defeat. (Ditka said, "Now I know how it feels to be on the other end of a blowout.") There was one vivid moment when the old Payton suddenly seemed reborn. He took a screen pass, evaded two defenders, cut past another, then turned and bulled into a covey of tacklers and was hit hard, helmet to helmet. This time Payton didn't jump up as he always did in the past. He was down on one knee, dazed, and had to leave the game for a few plays.

Payton didn't dwell on the embarrassing loss to San Francisco. A few days later he was notified that the first annual Walter Payton Trophy for the best player in I-AA college football went to Colgate's Kenny Gamble. It was predicted the award would rank second in prestige only to the Heisman Trophy. He also had to prepare himself for an emotional farewell. The following Sunday he would play his last regular home game against the Seattle Seahawks. That same week Bears' President Michael McCaskey announced that Payton had accepted an administrative position with the team. His job wasn't identified, but McCaskey said, "It's with an eye toward his dream of eventually owning an NFL franchise."

The day of the Seahawk game, the National Broadcasting Company's show *NFL Live* had a tribute to Payton. The commentary and interview were by Ahmad Rashad, a former great receiver with the Minnesota Vikings. He said he faced Payton twice a season for many years as a division opponent. Films of Payton in action were shown and Rashad spoke of his formidable ability:

"He was one of those rare players you couldn't help admiring even when he was beating hell out of you. He is the consummate superstar."

Payton talked of his feelings about retirement:

"It really didn't hit me until a couple of weeks ago. It was my last appearance in Minnesota and they introduced me. I spotted a girl's sign—'You're going to be missed. We love you, Walter.' It made my eyes a little wet."

Asked what he wanted to take out of the game, Payton's reply was somewhat unexpected: "I hurt. I cry. I bleed. I'm a normal person. I want to leave with what I came in with—my mental ability and physical capacity."

On December 20, 1987, Soldier Field was jammed with noisy, loving fans. The announcer for the brief ceremony held up his hands to quiet the crowd. Then, like a circus ringmaster presenting the star turn, his voice blared from the loudspeakers around the stadium: "Ladies and Gentlemen! Playing his 95th regular and final home game at Soldier Field—from Jackson State—Number 34—WALTER PAYTON!"

Payton, without his helmet but wearing his trademark white headband, walked slowly out on the field to a thunderous ovation. He was joined at the 50-yard line by his wife, two children, mother, brother, and his high school and college coaches. He was presented with an oil portrait of himself. Chicago's Mayor, Eugene Sawyer, hung the city's Medal of Merit around his neck. Michael McCaskey then made the announcement everyone was waiting for:

"I cannot imagine another Chicago Bear wearing number 34. When you finish playing, number 34 will be retired. You are the greatest running back to ever play the game of football. Walter, we love you. Thank you for enriching our lives."

Payton's eyes were cloudy when he spoke to the crowd: "I never thought it would end this way. The hardest thing is to say good-bye to the ones I love. Those guys standing down there in the end zone are the ones I love. The only thing I can say now is thanks for being here. Thank you."

"Those guys" he referred to were his teammates. It was a bittersweet good-bye. Rising to the occasion, Payton had probably his best game of the year. He rushed for 79 yards on 17 carries, caught 2 passes for 20 yards, and scored two touchdowns. But it was in a lost cause. Chicago, playing without Jim McMahon, was beaten 34–21. It was the first time they had lost two games in a row since 1984.

Fate would determine how much longer Payton played football and whether he would make it to a second Super Bowl. It depended on how far Chicago, no longer a dominant team, could go in the playoffs. Payton had one more regular game to chase another Jim Brown record. He needed only 2 more scores to tie Brown's 126 total touchdowns lifetime, running and receiving. In the pressbox after the Seahawks game, a writer remarked that he was sure Payton wasn't thinking much about another record at this stage of his career. Another writer gave him a sly smile.

"Don't bet on it. Don't ever bet against Walter Payton, no matter what he tries."

The Monday after the game it was announced that Neal Anderson would miss the final game against the Los Angeles Raiders because of a knee injury. There was no decision yet whether he would miss the playoffs. Everyone began to speculate about Payton's role. . . .

Perhaps he would once again—in an astonishing last hurrah—lead the Bears, be their force and spirit as he had for so many years. It was not beyond him.

Before the Raiders game, someone on the broadcasting

staff called Jim Brown and asked how he'd feel if Payton tied his record. He said he'd be happy and wanted "Walter to go for it." But no man, not even Payton, has a guarantee of heroic endings. He gained more rushing yardage than he had all season—82 on 20 carries, and caught 2 passes for 21—but didn't score. With only 1:31 left to play, Chicago had a slim 6–3 lead and only needed to run out the clock. Payton took the handoff from the quarterback and started to sweep right. Raider defenders broke through and had him pinned near the sideline. He tried to pivot and run for open ground. A year or two before, he might have made it. But as he swung around, a tackler knocked the ball loose and the Raiders recovered on the 50-yard line.

Everyone knew Payton had made a mistake. He should have taken the hit and gone down to run time off the clock, but his instinct was to claw for every yard or two. What was a heroic virtue now seemed like an ironic flaw. But the Bears held and the Raiders lost the ball on downs without getting close enough to try for the tying field goal. It would be a sad memory of his last carry in a regular season game. John Madden, broadcasting the game that day, had called Payton the "best ever" running back in football history. When Payton fumbled, there was a noticeable falter in his voice. Later that night, Pete Axthelm, a cable television commentator and notorious Raiders fan, said he screamed at the Raiders, hated them when they recovered the fumble. No one, he said, should have made Walter Payton go out that way. The reaction of both men was typical of the respect and love everyone had for him.

12

THE BEARS WERE SCHEDULED TO MEET the Washington Redskins on January 10, 1988, in their first playoff game. Three days before the possible end of his 13th and final season—or three weeks from the end he would prefer, in Super Bowl XXII—Walter Payton had one more fantasy.

"There's three seconds left in the game. We're on their 20-yard-line, down by five points. I run the ball for a touchdown and we end up winning the game. And when I run into the end zone and throw the ball down—I just fly off—Whooooooosh!"

He meant upward, and his arm extended in a deep climb like a fighter pilot demonstrating a tactic. His number had been retired, and he had said his formal, public good-byes. But now came the cruel business that could define the success or failure of a season—playoff games where a loss eliminated a team from further play. The injury to Neal Anderson had once again placed the burden on Payton. His records, the numbers, were the past. His increased importance to the Bears came at the climax of a season when, for the first time in his career, he was the second-leading rusher on his team.

"There were times it was frustrating," he said, "and there were times it was jubilant. Over the years I've had to adjust and adapt to change. To say the least, it's been a very educational and enlightening year for me. I'm glad it happened."

Early in the week before the Washington game, Payton was asked if he thought that this game might be his last.

"Not at all. You can't think about that. But I don't think this will be my last game. I don't see any reason why it should be my last game."

The year before, in a 27–13 playoff loss to Washington, Payton had gained only 38 yards on 14 carries, the second lowest of his career in a playoff game. He had also lost one fumble. His lowest playoff yardage—the 32 he gained in the NFC championship victory over the Rams in 1985—was overshadowed by the Bears' powerful defense. Later that month he didn't score a touchdown in the Super Bowl win against New England. Now, with the added drama of his farewell season winding down, he had a last chance to be a force.

"I think everybody likes to be challenged, for their skills and their talents to be pushed to the limit. It brings out the best in you. I'm no different than anybody else. I like the competition. I also like to win."

The game against the Redskins was played on a day when the wind chill was well below zero, customary Chicago weather in January. The Bears jumped out to a 7–0 lead in the first quarter. Doug Williams, Washington's quarterback, fumbled on his 30-yard line as he was sacked by Bears' defensive end Richard Dent. The Bears recovered and Payton was given the ball on the first carry. Behind a crushing block by Matt Suhey, he gained 15 yards. He ran again for 7 yards. After a Suhey gain, fullback Calvin Thomas took the ball into the end zone. Chicago scored again in the second quarter on a pass from Jim McMahon to Ron Morris. Chicago closed down the Redskin running game and it began to look like a runaway. With Suhey, a punishing blocker, to spring him, Payton ripped off good gains on almost every carry. He showed flashes of his old brilliance, calling on some inner resource, his powerful legs churning for that extra yard. But by the end of the first half, a courageous Redskin team had tied the score.

Only a few minutes into the second half, the game turned. The Chicago punter got off his best kick of the game. The Redskins' returner, Darrell Green, the fastest man in the league, caught the ball over his shoulder at his 48-yard-line, close to the sideline. Fifteen yards downfield, Green cut to his left, directly into the path of a hurtling Bear tackler. Green never broke stride and never hesitated. He hurdled the tackler and outran the pursuit for a touchdown and a 21–14 lead. A Chicago field goal closed it to 21–17, with 20 minutes still left in the game. But after gaining 74 yards on 13 carries in the first half, Payton was stopped by the stout Redskin defense, gaining only 11 yards on 5 carries the rest of the game. McMahon, playing poorly after reinjuring a shoulder and hamstring, threw three interceptions in the second half.

Chicago had one last chance, with a little over a minute to play. They started from their own 48-yard-line, but three plays gained only 2 yards. On 4th and 8 yards for a 1st down, McMahon went with his best. He tossed a swing pass to Payton, circling to the right. He started downfield, but with 31 seconds left to play he was knocked out of bounds at the Redskin 43-yard-line. Payton, after all the years and all the yards—as almost every sportswriter in America would write—came up a yard short. It was the last time he would carry the ball in the National Football League. The Redskins took over and Doug Williams ran out the last seconds by taking the snap from center and kneeling.

"I had to get out of bounds because we were out of time-outs," Payton said later. "But I was trying to get the first down. I was trying to get as much as I possibly could. I just fell a little short."

When the game ended, players from both teams rushed from the frozen field for the warm locker rooms. Payton was suddenly struck by the finality—the end of his career—and he was reluctant to leave. He sat alone on the Bears' bench, head in his hands and crying.

"One more year," someone yelled from the stands. "One more year, Walter, you can do it."

The crowd refused to leave until he did and picked up the chant—"*WAL-ter* . . . *WAL-ter*. . . ."

"We love you, Walter," a woman yelled.

Payton looked up finally, his face streaked with tears. After about ten minutes he rose slowly and walked off the field, followed by cameramen and reporters until he disappeared into the tunnel leading to the Bears' locker room. Inside, he moved through the crowd of newsmen and, still in helmet and full uniform, sat on a bench in front of his locker, his eyes closed. The reporters respected his silence and waited. Calvin Thomas at the next locker watched Payton for several minutes, then bent close:

"You all right?"

"Yeah, I'm fine." Payton opened his eyes. "I'm just gonna take my time. This is the last time I'll take it off."

Payton began to remove his uniform, slowly, almost cere-moniously, like a knight shedding his armor after the last

Walter Payton after the final game of his career, January 10, 1988. The Bears had lost to the Washington Redskins by a score of 21–17. *Courtesy of Wide World Photos.*

joust. But the greatest running back in NFL history merited every bit of theatrics in his last show. He took off his gray thermal gloves, helmet, jersey, and shoulder pads. Still wearing a navy blue hood, he tore the white tape from his shoes and cut the tape from both ankles. He took the thigh pads from his white uniform pants and held them up to show the crowd.

"Tell you what," he said, "these go all the way back to high school."

"Give them to me," said Ken Valdiserri, a Bears' publicity man. "I'll send them to the Hall of Fame."

Payton smiled for the first time. "Three years of high school, four years of college, thirteen years here, I've worn the same thigh pads. Something, huh?"

He stripped and showered and when he returned to his locker and began dressing, Bill Gleason, a veteran Chicago newsman, said:

"You gonna miss me?"

Payton grinned. "You gonna miss *me*?"

"Absolutely." Gleason gestured to the crowd of reporters. "You gonna miss this?"

"No, not too bad. But I'll miss you. What do you remember most?"

"How much fun you were."

"That's the reason I was playing," Payton said. "It was fun."

Payton polished his black cowboy boots with a towel. "Got to look the part," he said and grinned.

Someone asked him about staying on the field so long after the game ended.

"I knew it was going to happen. I just didn't want to force it."

He paused, then said his farewell as a player to the reporters.

"The last thirteen years there were a lot of good moments and a lot of bad moments. There were times when you didn't want to quit and times when you could see quit in sight. Over all, it's been a lot of fun. When you take away the fun, it's time to leave. That's why it's so hard to leave now. It's still fun. God's been very good to me. I'm truly blessed."

Across the room, Jim McMahon told a reporter: "I'm gonna miss him in the backfield. I'm gonna miss him in the locker room. I'm gonna miss being around the guy. The day he walks out of football is the day he should walk into the Hall of Fame. The hell with that bleeping waiting five years."

It was time for Walter Payton to leave. Like any hero of legend, he walked off into an appropriate sunset outside Soldier Field.

In the words of New York *Times* sports columnist, Dave Anderson—"And despite what happened on his last play, he was never a yard short."

They will be playing football on Sundays in Chicago. But the games will be just a little less elegant. A little less exciting. A little less sweet.

WALTER PAYTON'S
NATIONAL FOOTBALL LEAGUE RECORDS

Rushing Yards, Career—16,726
Rushing Attempts, Career—3,838
Combined Attempts (Rushing, Receiving, Kick Returns)—4,347
Combined Yards, Career—21,803
Rushing Yards, One Game—275 (1977)
Rushing Touchdowns, Career—110
Games Rushing 100 or More Yards—77
Rushing 1,000 or More Yards, Seasons—10 (1976–81, 1983–86)
Most Pass Receptions by Back, Career—476

RECORDS PAYTON IS TIED FOR FIRST

Consecutive Seasons Leading League, Attempts—4 (1976–79)
Consecutive Seasons Rushing 1,000 or More Yards—6 (1976–81)

PAYTON'S STANDING IN OTHER RECORDS

Most Total Touchdowns—125—Second
Consecutive Games 100 or More Yards—9 (1985)—Tied Second
Most Seasons Leading League, Attempts—4 (1976–79)—Tied
    Second
Most Games 200 or More Yards, Season—2 (1977)—Tied Third
Most Games 200 or More Yards, Career—2—Tied Fifth
Most Games 100 or More Yards, Season—10 (1977)—Tied Sixth

Walter Payton averaged 5.1 yards gained every time he ran or
caught the ball or completed a pass in regular season games.

INDEX

143

145

147